Introduction to Information Visualization

D1559507

Riccardo Mazza

Introduction to Information Visualization

 Springer

Riccardo Mazza
University of Lugano
Switzerland

ISBN: 978-1-84800-218-0   e-ISBN: 978-1-84800-219-7
DOI: 10.1007/978-1-84800-219-7

British Library Cataloguing in Publication Data
A catalogue record for this book is available from the British Library

Library of Congress Control Number: 2008942431

Printed on acid-free paper

Springer Science+Business Media
springer.com

To Vincenzo and Giulia

Preface

Imagine having to make a car journey. Perhaps you're going to a holiday resort that you're not familiar with. Your wife has been really eager to go. Spending the holidays in an appealing destination will certainly make her happy and it would go a long way toward rewarding her for the daily struggle of keeping the children under control, and even they could do with a change of scenery every now and again. Luckily, you have your trusty laptop at hand. You connect to the Internet (and who doesn't have an Internet connection these days) and log on to a well-known website that will show you exactly which route you should drive to reach your longed-for destination. The site is extremely efficient: Not only does it show, in meticulous detail, the course to follow (even the crossroads are accurately indicated), but it even provides you with a detailed map highlighting the advised route.

And you? Will you have to surrender your hobby for two weeks: golf? Never. Consulting the map provided by the website, you discover that, on the way to the highly anticipated getaway location, you will pass just 20 kilometers from an area that boasts one of the finest golf courses. But that's not all—you zoom into the area and find out that there are some interesting tourist spots that hadn't come up before due to the overly large scale of the map. You learn that there is a 19th-century castle nearby that offers relaxing weekends with beauty and spa treatments and provides a babysitting service to take care of your children all day, entertaining them with games, songs, and a variety of amusements. It's done: You've planned your journey and, thanks to the opportunity offered by the website, you have had the chance to please your family, without having to forgo your hobby.

All of this thanks to a website? Of course not. All the site offered you was a detailed map that featured, in addition to the route leading to your destination, a selection of information on the location, attractions, and places of interest in the area. These places of interest aren't necessarily found precisely along the route indicated by the ultra-efficient website: They could indeed be a short distance from your path but capture your interest nonetheless, as seen in the case presented here. But at what distance? And what sort of location might I be interested in? The situation just described illustrates a typical case in which the use of a graphical representation has taken on a decisive role in the discovery of new information. How can I go about representing a series of various types of information that is complex by nature, linked together by a relationship of "proximity" that may be very vague and imprecise? (When are two locations deemed near? Are two locations near when they're 20 kilometers from each other? And if they were 60 kilometers from each other, would they still be considered close?). How can I communicate to the users of my website which of the "nearby" locations might be of some artistic or architectural interest? And what if they are just interested in finding out which route to take?

In these circumstances, the use of graphical representations mediated by the computer can help in the analysis of and search for "imprecise" information. Imprecision is not in the nature of data (which in itself is precise) but rather by the type of search and interest that a generic user may not have made very clear beforehand. The "let's look at the graphics and then see what to do" situation is one of the *modus operandi* in which the graphical representation of information is at its best, as portrayed in the previous case. We don't know what to look for; therefore, we try to represent everything we possibly can, to then examine the information and come to a decision ("Along the way you pass close to a golf course? Then we can spend the weekend there!"), demonstrate a hypothesis ("The alternative path the website suggested indeed shorter in terms of kilometers, but requires crossing a mountain pass at an altitude of more than 1,000 meters. Therefore, the traveling time required is greater"), or even communicate an idea effectively ("See? If we stop here, we'll be at the halfway mark. We'll let the kids rest for a day and then set off again much more relaxed").

This book illustrates such concepts in a simple and thorough manner. It aims to build a reference for the situations in which the graphical representation of information, generated and assisted by computer, can be helpful in carrying out explorative analysis on the data, effectively communicating ideas, data, or concepts, and helping to demonstrate or disprove a hypothesis on data.

Created as a support text for a university course, this book is also suitable for a wide and heterogeneous reading audience. It contains suggestions for setting communication systems based on or availing of graphical representations. The text will, above all, illustrate cases, situations, tools, and methods that can help make the graphical representation of information effective and efficient.

Lugano, October 2008   *Riccardo Mazza*

Acknowledgments

I would like to thank all the people who have contributed to this book in the various phases of its development, in particular, Enrico Bertini, Giuseppe Santucci, Daniele Galiffa, and Francesca Morganti for their helpful comments and suggestions. Special thanks to Lynsey Dreaper for helping with the translation from the first version in Italian. I would also like to thank all the authors and publishers of the copyrighted materials included in this book for their kind permission to reproduce the images.

Finally, I would like to thank my wife, Beatrice, for her support, encouragement, and understanding during the many late nights spent working on this book.

Contents

List of Figures

Chapter 1
Introduction to Visual Representations

Let's stop for a moment and consider just how much information we have to take in every day as part of our routine activities. E-mails arrive on our computers, credit card statements arrive from the bank every month, and last-minute holiday offers, stock market index variations, and advertising leaflets fill the mailbox. Not to mention work. Perhaps you work in a large department store and have to decide the discount policies to be applied to sale items: Which items should we put on sale in the coming months? Summer is arriving—should we perhaps put the beach umbrellas on sale? What percentage discount should we apply? How did the sales of the previous month's promotional items go?

In all of these situations, the common recurring theme is the enormous quantity of information that we have to deal with on a daily basis. Each of the previously described situations almost always involves making a decision: Which e-mail or advertising flyer can we throw out because it doesn't interest us? How much did we charge to the credit card last month? Will we perhaps need to limit our spending in the future? Where can we spend the next holiday without it costing us a fortune? Would it be worthwhile to invest our savings in a particular stock? What discount can we put on the beach umbrellas in the coming months?

Perhaps we haven't even realized, but in the last decade, the quantity of information that we all have to process has increased enormously. The globalization of economy and communication, but above all the rapid advances in technology (and not only communication and information technology), have brought us in, recent years, to what some noted scholars define as *information pollution*. Anyway, if we really think about it, what we are witnessing in reality is not an explosion of information, but rather an explosion of *data*, which we are continuously pressed to observe, process, and develop, for our family or work activities. We are *informed* by the data that we continually receive from numerous sources. The information, very valuable and important for our lives, is built and elaborated on starting from this continuous and constant influx of data that we are passively or actively subjected to. Therefore, we need effective methods that allow us to go through this information and, for example, help us make decisions.

R. Mazza, *Introduction to Information Visualization*,
DOI: 10.1007/978-1-84800-219-7_1, © Springer-Verlag London Limited 2009

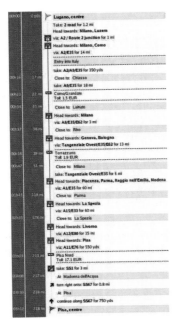 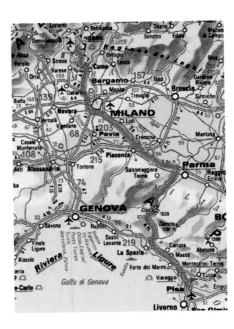

Fig. 1.1 Road map for the Lugano–Pisa route, provided in a textual version (left) and a visual version (right). Image from http://www.viamichelin.com; reproduced with the permission of Via-Michelin.

There are numerous situations in which we use visual representations to understand the various data. This could involve anything from last week's stock market trends to a travel itinerary or even the weather forecast for various geographical areas. Thanks to our visual perception ability, a visual representation is often more effective than written text.

Let's take, for instance, the case of a person who has to travel by car from Lugano to Pisa and needs to find out which route to take. It is possible to represent this information in a textual form by providing, for example, a meticulous description of the roads to follow and the junctions to take. It is, however, also possible to represent this information in a visual form, through a map that visually highlights the entire route to follow. A route generated by a very popular website is represented in Fig. 1.1.

The website in Fig. 1.1 provides a very useful service. We can set a departure point and a destination, and the website will indicate the route to follow. Among the various configurable options, we can request an itinerary that favors the highway or the toll-free roads. The website creates the best route possible, according to our requirements. The route, as we can see in Fig. 1.1, is presented in two forms: One is a textual table that reports the distances, the names of the roads to follow, and the junctions to note, and the other is a visual version in the form of a road map.

The website provides two complementary versions that can be used for different purposes. For example, a truck driver transporting goods will want to know exactly which roads to take and their relative distances; in this case, the textual version can be very useful. There are, however, some aspects that can be interesting when we plan an itinerary for a recreational journey, such as the possibility of finding an alternative route or places close to the route that might be of interest to the tourist. Although useless for the truck driver, these aspects could indeed be indispensable for a family wishing to program the route for their next holiday and can be effectively revealed through the use of the visual version of the route.

The visual version has the advantage of using some graphical properties that are very quickly and efficiently processed by visual perception. The visual attributes like color, size, proximity, and movement are immediately taken in and processed by the perceptual ability of vision, even before the complex cognitive processes of the human mind come into play.

Let's clarify this concept with an example. Figure 1.2 shows a sequence of numerical data and a visual representation, constructed by horizontal lines of length proportional to the values on the left that they represent.

320

260

380

280

420

400

Fig. 1.2 Mapping numerical values to the lengths of bars.

Let's suppose that we have to determine the maximum and minimum numerical values indicated on the left. If we didn't have the lines at our disposal, we would have to perform the following procedure: Read each of the numerical values, keeping in mind the extreme values (the maximum and the minimum) that we come across while reading them, right through to the end. In one sense this is a cognitive exercise, since it is necessary to compare the pairs of numerical values each time to decide if one value is higher or lower than the other.

We'll repeat the same exercise, this time with the aid of the lines on the right. The length of the lines shows us at a glance the maximum and minimum values. This information is processed by our visual perception, which immediately recognizes the lengths of the lines and arranges them in relationship to the values represented.

Since humans perceive *visual attributes* very well, like the extension of the lines in the previous case, we can represent a great deal of different data by "mapping" them to different visual attributes. For instance, we could represent the lines of the previous figure with different colors, or different widths, to codify further data. In this case, the visual representations, if well constructed, can be useful not only for perceiving information more quickly but also for processing several items of information at the same time. Let's not forget that the human brain is a "machine" that constantly processes a huge amount of data and information simultaneously. In this way we can easily single out, in one or more collections of data, the maximum and minimum values, the existence of relationships between the data, grouping, trends, gaps, or interesting values. As a result, the visual representations allow us to understand complex systems, make decisions, and find information that otherwise might remain hidden in the data.

1.1 Presentation

When we want to communicate an idea, we sometimes use a picture. It could be a sketch on paper, a drawing on a blackboard, or images projected on a slide or transparency. The visual representations help us to illustrate concepts that, if expressed verbally, we would find difficult to explain clearly to a listener. Just imagine trying to explain to someone over the telephone how to fix a bathroom faucet. When we have data with which we need to illustrate concepts, ideas, and properties intrinsic to that data, the use of visual representation offers us a valid communication tool. The difficult part is in defining the representations that effectively achieve their goal. Edward Tufte, one of the major contemporary scholars of this discipline and Professor Emeritus of Political Science, Statistics, and Computer Science at Yale University, maintains that "excellence in statistical graphics consists of complex ideas communicated with clarity, precision, and efficiency" [58]. It is necessary for a picture to give the reader as much data as can be processed quickly, using as little space as possible.

Let's look at the visual representation illustrated in Fig. 1.3. It deals with a map created by Charles Joseph Minard, a French engineer, in 1869. The map was conceived to illustrate the number of losses suffered by Napoleon's army during the disastrous march toward Moscow in 1812. The thick band shows the route taken by the troupes, from the Polish border to Moscow, and the width of this track represents the number of soldiers present at each point of the journey. The number of losses suffered by the army is evident at a glance. Of the 422,000 soldiers who set off from the Polish border, only 100,000 arrived in Moscow. Napoleon's retreat during the freezing Russian winter is represented by the dark line, linked to a graph that reports the harsh temperatures that further decimated the already-exhausted army. Some rivers, in which numerous soldiers lost their lives attempting to cross, are also

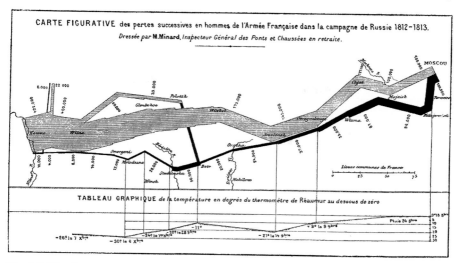

Fig. 1.3 Visual representation of the march of Napoleon's army in the Russian campaign of 1812, produced by Charles J. Minard.

indicated. This visual is a superb example of the concept of excellence expressed by Tufte, who, not without good reason, defined it as "the best statistical graphic ever drawn" [58].

1.2 Explorative Analysis

The explorative analysis of data is one of the applications that benefits the most from visual representations and the ability of analysis by visual perception and the human cognitive system. This has been used for years to identify properties, relationships, regularities, or patterns. Jacques Bertin (a French cartographer who, as early as 1967, wrote a work defining the basic elements of every visual representation) defines it as "the visual means of resolving logical problems" [5].

We'll illustrate the concept with an example. Figure 1.4 displays some statistical data on cancer-related mortality among men in the United States in the period from 1970 to 1994. In the picture, the counties are represented (3,055 in total) by a color scale ranging from blue to red, according to the percentage of cases found in each county. Thanks to the color, we can single out the geographical areas with an average (white), below-average (blue shades), and above-average (red shades), number of cases. It is noticeable how above average-cases are predominantly found in the counties along the East Coast and in the south east of the United States. The American National Cancer Institute produced this and many other images with the aim of identifying possible causes for the onset of tumors. In fact, it is by now almost certain that most cases of cancer are associated in some way with lifestyles that

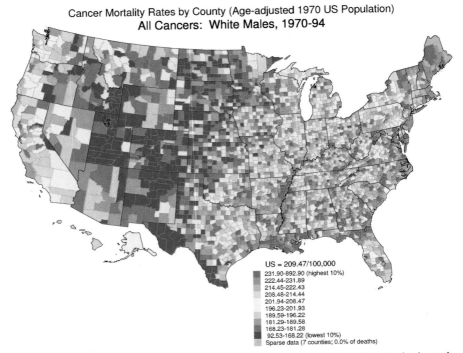

Cancer Mortality Rates by County (Age-adjusted 1970 US Population)
All Cancers: White Males, 1970-94

US = 209.47/100,000
231.90-892.90 (highest 10%)
222.44-231.89
214.45-222.43
208.48-214.44
201.94-208.47
196.23-201.93
189.59-196.22
181.29-189.58
168.23-181.28
92.53-168.22 (lowest 10%)
Sparse data (7 counties; 0.0% of deaths)

Fig. 1.4 A map of the United States showing the number of cancer related deaths in the male population from 1970 to 1994, subdivided into counties. Image from http://www3.cancer.gov/atlas/ and reproduced with permission.

people lead and other environmental factors. The representation in Fig. 1.4 does not provide an explanation as to why the incidence of death is higher in certain counties than in others but can suggest that researchers carry out epidemiological studies in determined regions, which may throw some light on factors that increase the risk of cancer. For instance, in the past, thanks to a visual representation of this type, a high number of cases of lung cancer were found in the coastal areas of Georgia, Virginia, north east Florida, and Louisiana. Researchers found that these cases were connected to asbestos powder, inhaled by workers in the shipyards during the Second World War.

1.3 Confirmative Analysis

Visual representation is also a visual means of carrying out confirmative analysis on structural relationships between series of data, to confirm or infirm hypotheses on the data. For example, stock market workers are well aware that the stock exchange of various nations is influenced by events. This can be illustrated by Fig.

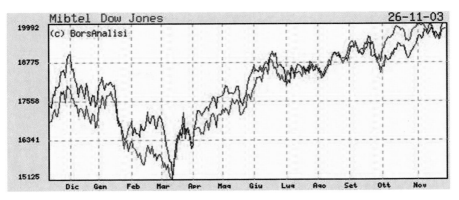

Fig. 1.5 A picture that compares the Italian MIBTEL stock market share index (in blue) to the U.S. Dow Jones shares index (in red). Image from http://www.borsanalisi.com and reproduced with permission.

1.5, where the values of the Italian stock market index MIBTEL and those of the American Dow Jones are represented over the course of a year. In the figure, it is easily noticeable how, when compared to one another, the rising and falling phases of the two stock markets follow a similar trend. This correlation between the two indexes, clearly represented by a picture, could be demonstrated through the use of complicated math formulas, which would certainly be less expressive and intuitive than a picture.

1.4 Information Visualization

Eminent authors often refer to visual or graphical representations by the term *visualization* (or *visualisation* in the less common British version of the term). In this text, we use the expression *visual representation* rather than other synonyms. Obviously, this is not a casual choice; we use the terminology that is most in keeping with the subject at hand.

Spence [54] has noted that there is a wide range of uses for the term *visualization*. A quick check in a dictionary reveals that "visualization" is an activity in which humans beings are engaged as an internal construction in the mind [54, 65]. It is something that cannot be printed on paper or displayed on a computer screen. Taking this into consideration, we can summarize that visualization is a cognitive activity, facilitated by external visual representations from which people build an internal mental representation of the world [54, 65]. Computers may facilitate the visualization process with some visualization tools. This has been especially true in recent years with the use of increasingly powerful, low-cost computers. However, the above definition is independent from computers: Although computers can facilitate visualization, it still remains an activity that occurs in the mind. Some authors use the term "visualization" to refer to both the printed visual representation and the cognitive process of understanding an image. In this book, we maintain the distinction between the creation of a pictorial representation of some data and the cognitive process that takes place when interpreting the pictorial representation.

In this text, we don't speak of generic visual representation, which could be a figure that explains how to calculate the length of a cathetus in a right triangle:

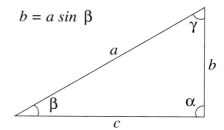

Fig. 1.6 Example of a visual representation that explains how to calculate the cathetus of a right triangle.

Instead, we are interested in visually representing data that can be generated, calculated, or found in many diverse ways, such as data from soccer matches in the last championship, data on the evolution of the population in various nations of the world, data revealed by instruments for environmental pollution tests, etc. The objective is to be informed by this data, or to put together information through the analysis (visual) of the data. The expression *information visualization* was coined by the researchers of Xerox PARC at the end of the 1980s to distinguish a new discipline concerned with the creation of visual artifacts aimed at amplifying cognition.

1.5 From Data to Wisdom

But just how is information created from the data that we represent in visual form? We have already mentioned that we are constantly solicited by a great amount of data arriving from numerous sources. In his essay in *Information Design* [29], Nathan Shedroff analyzes how the process of understanding data comes about, which we can outline in Fig. 1.7.

Shedroff defines this process as the "continuum of understanding" and describes it as a continuum that generates information from data. In addition, the information can be transformed into knowledge and finally into wisdom. Let's look at the principal features of the process:

- **Data** are entities that, of themselves, lack any meaning. They constitute the "bricks" with which we build information and our communicative processes. Let's take the example of data on the consumer price index (CPI) that are provided monthly by the national institute of statistics. These are a collection of numbers that taken singularly, are not much use to the general public. It is, how-

Fig. 1.7 The continuum of understanding, according to Nathan Shedroff.

ever, precisely these data on which the institute bases its annual report on the state of the economy and the nation's inflation.

- Data alone are not enough to establish a communicative process. To give meaning to this data, they must first be processed, organized, and presented in a suitable format. This transformation and manipulation of the data produces **information** that "is accomplished by organizing it into a meaningful form, presenting it in meaningful and appropriate ways, and communicating the context around it" [29]. When the institute of statistics website provides us with data from the last five years, arranged into months and with comparisons and annual averages, we are able to establish the instances of inflation on the consumer price index of the past year and to understand how they compare to preceding years. This information is made possible through the organization (also in the form of tables and averages calculated at the end of the year) of the statistical data assembled. At this stage, the information is conceived.
- When information is integrated with experience, it creates **knowledge**. When we have experiences, we acquire the knowledge with which we are able to understand things. Think of a student, for example, who has to complete exercises on a topic that the teacher has explained. The exercises need to stimulate and challenge the student with problems to solve, so that the theoretical concepts can be applied and called upon in real-life situations. The development of knowledge should be the principal aim of any communication process.
- **Wisdom** is the highest level of comprehension. It can be defined as the stage in which a person has acquired such an advanced level of knowledge of processes and relationships (Shedroff calls it "meta-knowledge") that it is then possible to express qualified judgment on data. Wisdom is self-induced through contemplation, the study and interpretation of knowledge, but, unlike knowledge, it cannot be directly transmitted or taught.

Information visualization is located between data and information. It provides the methods and tools with which to organize and represent the data to finally produce information. Historically considered as a sector of the information discipline commonly known as "human–computer interaction," only in the past 10 years has it been considered a discipline in itself. In Card et al. [8] it is defined as "the use of computer-supported, interactive, visual representations of data to amplify cognition." Basically, the cognitive human processes create information taken from the data presented to us; we wish to improve the cognitive process precisely through visual representation of this data, making use of the perceptual ability of the human visual system. The widespread availability of increasingly powerful and less expensive computers, combined with advances in computer graphics, has made it possible for everyone to have access to systems with which to interact, manipulate visual representations in real time, and explore data that are displayed in various forms and representations.

1.6 Mental Models

Visual representations help us to understand data and therefore produce better information. But how does all of this come about? Robert Spence [54] stresses the fact that the process of visualizing data (meaning the activity of a person who observes a visual representation of content) is a cognitive activity with which people build *mental models* of data, or rather an internal representation of the world around them, from which they manage to expand on and understand such data. It's something that cannot be printed on a sheet of paper or visualized on a computer screen. Just what is a mental model then?

The term "mental model" was first used by Kenneth Craik in 1943 in his book *The Nature of Explanation* [15] and is mainly used by cognitive psychology scholars to describe how humans build knowledge from the world around them. Cognitive psychology defines it as a sort of "internal codification" to the brain of the outside world. The formation of an internal model is aided by visual properties that help us to build a "visual map" of the data that are shown. For example, if we often take the route described in Fig. 1.1, after the first time we no longer need to consult the map, because in our mind we have already created an internal model of the route to follow. This does not mean that we have memorized a copy of the map or the table in Fig. 1.1, but that we can recognize the main reference points (for example, the names of the cities, highways, and intersections) that we have associated with our mental model.

Card et al. [8] explained how visual representations can boost cognitive process, because they allow some inferences to be done very easily for humans. For instance, if, during a journey from Lugano to Pisa, we wish to stop twice to rest, at about one third and two thirds along the way, we can immediately identify two locations by consulting the visual representation of the route.

In their article "Why a diagram is (sometimes) worth ten thousand words" [38], Larkin and Simon carried out an empirical study comparing, in solving physics problems, diagrams versus the equivalent textual descriptions. The conclusion is that the diagrams are expressively more effective due to three properties:

1. **Locality**. In every visual representation, each element has its place in the physical space. In a well-designed representation, two pieces of data, which have to
   be processed simultaneously, can be represented by two different visual elements
   positioned in the immediate spatial vicinity. For example, in Fig. 1.5, the historical values of two different stock market indexes are placed together in a single
   diagram. This allows the reader to compare their fluctuations directly.
2. **Minimizing labeling**. This property is linked to the ability of human beings to
   recognize information represented in a visual format, without the need for a detailed description in textual form. It is better still if this information resembles,
   as much as possible, the actual world that it seeks to represent. The map shown
   in Fig. 1.1, for example, uses precise visual properties, such as the lines with the
   double red stripes at the edges and yellow at the center to denote the highway,
   while the suggested route is highlighted with the color purple and is superim-
   posed on the highway to be followed. The junctions and exits to take (such as at
   Parma and La Spezia in the figure) are easily distinguished from the intersection
   of the two highways. The symbolic representations of the intersections that we
   find in the textual version, to the left of the map, are not necessary since they are
   already immediately understood from the visual version.
3. **Perceptual enhancement**. As previously cited, we can process a large amount
   of perceptual inference through visual representations, allowing us to single out
   relationships and dependence between data very naturally. For example, in Fig.
   1.4, it is easy to single out groupings (known as *clusters*) of counties with a high
   rate of cancer. It is also easy to individualize some counties in the center and north
   of the United States showing an abnormal situation: a high number of cases in
   these counties, compared to a low number of cases in neighbouring counties.

1.7 Scientific Visualization

When we have to visually represent data, we have to deal with the problem of their
nature. Data themselves can have a wide variety of forms, but we can distinguish
between data that have a physical correspondence and are closely related to mathematical structures and models (for example, the flow of air surrounding the wing of
an airplane during flight or the density of a hole in the ozone layer that surrounds the
earth), and data that have no correspondence with physical space and that we call
abstract. We have seen some examples of abstract data in the visual representations
described previously: the fluctuations in the stock market, the effect of the temperature on Napoleon's army during the retreat from Russia, the percentage of cancer
cases in U.S. counties. Despite its name, abstract data always deal with concrete
data, often resulting from some activity generated by humans, but don't correspond
to a physical object positioned in any part of space.

In cases in which we must deal with data that have a correspondence in physical
space, we speak of *scientific visualization*, while *information visualization* deals
with visualization of abstract data that don't necessarily have a spatial dimension.

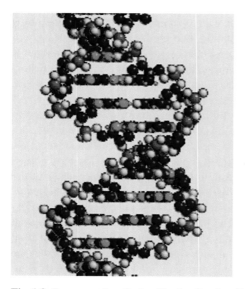 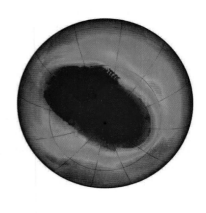

Fig. 1.8 Two examples of scientific visualization. To the left is a representation of a DNA structure, to the right the representation of the hole in the ozone layer over the South Pole on September 22, 2004. Images taken from the NASA Goddard Space Center archives and reproduced with permission.

Scientific visualization is a discipline that aims to visually represent the results of scientific experiments or natural phenomena (two examples are reported in Fig. 1.8). In this text, we deal predominantly with abstract data. For a complete treatment of scientific visualization, it is advisable to consult the *Visualization Handbook* by Hansen and Johnson [27].

1.8 Criteria for Good Visual Representations

What is it that distinguishes a good visual representation from a mediocre one? When can one speak of excellence in visual representation? Numerous scholars have set this challenge for themselves and have come up with the most disparate criteria. From a pragmatic standpoint, we can immediately say that visual representation is considered "good quality" when it fully satisfies the communication and analytic requirements of those for whom it was intended and created.

But how can we go from a collection of abstract data to a visual representation that both is meaningful to the data it represents and, at the same time, can be useful for acquiring new knowledge from that data? There is no magic formula that, given a collection of data, shows us systematically which type of representation to use. It depends on the nature of the data, the type of information that it seeks to represent, and its intended users. But more importantly, it depends on the experience, creativity, and competence of whoever designs the representation. In literature, we find many innovative ideas and proposals that, even if their validity has been demonstrated through empirical studies with potential users, have remained unpractised and haven't found any following in the commercial world.

1.8.1 Graphical Excellence

Edward Tufte is certainly the most prominent expert in the world of statistical graphics for all that involves the excellence of visual representation. His works *The Visual Display of Quantitative Information* [58], *Envisioning Information* [59], *Visual Explanations* [60], and his latest work, *Beautiful Evidence* [61], are true milestones in the field of statistical graphics. Tufte points out some criteria to follow to ensure that a visual representation is effective. According to Tufte, a good picture is a well-built presentation of "interesting" data. It is something that brings together substance, statistic, and design. It aims to clearly, precisely, and efficiently present and communicate complex ideas. More generally, it aims to provide the viewer with "the greatest number of ideas, in the shortest time, using the least amount of ink, in the smallest space" [58]. In the numerous examples that Tufte reports in these texts, it is shown how very often whoever realizes the visual representation has artistic, rather than statistical, competence. This has led to the loss of power (and credibility) of visual representations, reducing them to simply being decorative tools.

Stephen Few has interpreted the teachings of Edward Tufte and has published two very interesting texts: *Show Me the Numbers* [19] and *Information Dashboard Design* [20]. The first is directed at visual statistics professionals, while the second is useful for anyone who has to realize visual dashboards. Few's books are written in a very pragmatic style, useful for those who want to find tips and best practices for building excellent visual representations.

1.8.2 Graphical Integrity

Tufte and Bertin [58, 5] report numerous cases of visual representation that, more or less intentionally, may lead to wrong interpretations. Tufte emphasizes what he defines with the term "visual integrity": The picture should not in any way distort or create false interpretations of the data. The representation of numerical data, just as they are physically designed on the surface of the graphic, should be directly proportional to the numerical quantity represented. The variations of the data should be shown, not the variations of the picture. Furthermore, the number of dimensions of the image must not exceed the number of dimensions of the data. Even the legends are to be used without distortion and ambiguity. Very often the visual representations are designed by artists without any statistical competence; at times this may produce artistic artifacts rather than clear, direct, and unambiguous visual representations of data.

1.8.3 Maximize the Data–Ink Ratio

One of the criteria to which, according to Tufte, it is necessary to pay close attention is the quantity of elements present in a visual representation. It is important not to overload the reader with too much elements, which could end up being unnecessary, if not positively damaging, to the final learning. The presence of some useless decoration (borders, insets, backgrounds, 3D effects, etc.) or of superfluous perspective doesn't make the visual itself more attractive; in fact, it does no more than draw attention away from what the image seeks to communicate. Therefore, these visuals should always be avoided, as instead of illustrating data, they are merely artistic compositions. Primary importance is given to the exhibition of data, not to the visual.

To avoid the representation of redundant and useless information in the image, Tufte defines a very simple criterion on making the most of useful ink. Basically, it's necessary to calculate how much ink is used to represent, unambiguously and relevantly, the real data and compare it with the quantity of ink used to visually enrich the pictures with decorations and other visual elements. The following equation is provided:

$$data - ink\ ratio = \frac{data - ink}{total\ ink\ used}.$$

The aim is to maximize the data–ink ratio, eliminating any non essential elements. One way to do this is to review and redesign the graphic, gradually eliminating the decorative elements, the insets, the borders, and all of the visual elements not pertaining to the data. This is how visually clear information is created, simple to understand and consequentially more beautiful and elegant.

1.8.4 Aesthetics

Elegance in visuals is attained, according to Tufte, when the complexity of the data matches the simplicity of the design. It's not by mere chance that Tufte mentions Napoleon's march in the Russian campaign, as represented by Minard (see Fig. 1.3), as an example of visual elegance. Elegant visuals are professionally designed with great attention to detail, avoiding decorations lacking in content and choosing an appropriate format and design. Complex details should be easily accessible and used to display data.

1.9 Conclusion

In this chapter, we have introduced the discipline of information visualization as a means of helping humans represent and understand abstract data that may have no relation to the physical space around us. We have also shown how the visual representation of data may help in communicating, analyzing data, and confirming hypotheses.

Chapter 2
Creating Visual Representations

In this chapter, we'll take a closer look at the process of generating an artifact of visual representation, or rather the mechanism that creates a visual representation from a certain number of data, using specific computer processes. Without delving too far into technical details, we'll describe this process through a model that we will use as a reference for the interactive visual representation. Furthermore, we will present some common techniques for visualizing linear data structures.

2.1 A Reference Model

Let's imagine that we have at our disposal a collection of data on which we'd like to carry out explorative analysis to identify any possible unknown tendencies or relationships. How can we go about a creating visual representation from this data? As always, good design is the key to success in applications of this kind. Before tackling this delicate and extremely important aspect, however, we'll find out which tools information technology puts at our disposal to realize visual representations.

Computers can help us greatly and, if we don't want to attempt designing everything from scratch, these days there are many varieties of visualization software that can provide us with a complete series of visual templates. But how do these programs work?

Software dedicated to the creation of visual representation of abstract data, even if they differ greatly among themselves, all follow a generation process that can be outlined in Fig. 2.1. Let's take raw data as our starting point, or rather abstract data provided by the world around us. As we saw in the previous chapter, we speak of abstract data when these data don't necessarily have a specific connection with physical space. For example, they may deal with people's names, the prices of consumer products, voting results, and so on. These data are rarely available in a format that is suitable for treatment with automatic processing tools and, in particular, visualization software. Therefore, they must be processed appropriately, before being represented graphically.

R. Mazza, *Introduction to Information Visualization*,
DOI: 10.1007/978-1-84800-219-7_2, © Springer-Verlag London Limited 2009

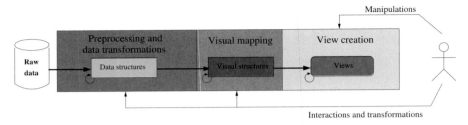

Fig. 2.1 The process of generating a graphical representation.

The creation of a visual artifact is a process that we can model through a sequence of successive stages:

1. preprocessing and data transformations,
2. visual mapping,
3. view creation.

We will describe each of these stages through an example, showing how data are transformed from the original format through to the creation of the visual representation.

2.1.1 Preprocessing and Data Transformations

We use the term "raw" to describe data supplied by the world around us. They can be data generated by tools, like the values of some polluting agents taken from a monitoring station during pollution testing. They can also be generated and calculated by appropriate software, such as weather forecast data. They may even be data linked to measurable events and entities that we find in nature or the social world, like the number of inhabitants or birth rates of the cities in a specific state. In each case, these collections of data (known as *datasets*) are very rarely supplied to us with a precise logical structure. To be able to process these data using software, we have to give them an organized logical structure. The structure usually used for this type of data is tabular—the arranging of data in a table—in a format appropriate for the software that must receive and process them. Sometimes the input data are contained in one or more databases and are, therefore, already available in electronic format and with a well-defined structure. In this case, the raw data correspond to the data located in the databases, and the phases of preprocessing and elaboration involve extracting these data from the database and converting them into the structured format used by the visualization software.

We'll show a concrete example, taken from [43]. Let us assume we want to study how people communicate in a discussion forum—the Internet-based communication tools that allow users to converse through an exchange of messages. The users can write a message on the forum, which all other users of the service can read.

Anyone can reply to the message, thus creating an environment of interactive discussion. Imagine having to carry out an analysis on data relative to the number of messages read and written in a discussion forum. Suppose, for instance, that we wish to quickly single out both the most active users (or, rather, those who read and write a high number of messages in the forum), as well as the users who silently read all of the messages and don't take an active part in the discussion. The tools that offer this type of service usually record every action carried out by the system's users in an appropriate file: the *log* file.

A typical log file of the discussions could have this format:

```
                             .
                             .
                             .
    [Tue 1 March 2005, 10:22 AM] Luigi "add post"
    [Tue 1 March 2005, 10:26 AM] Orazio "view discussion"
    [Tue 1 March 2005, 11:02 AM] Luigi "add post"
    [Tue 1 March 2005, 02:02 PM] Enzo "view discussion"
    [Tue 1 March 2005, 02:04 PM] Enzo "view discussion
                             .
                             .
                             .
```

This file will be the source of row data in our system. The preprocessing phase should convert these data into a tabular format.

The data structures can also be enriched with additional information or preliminary processing. In particular, **filtering** operations to eliminate unnecessary data and **calculations** for obtaining new data, such as statistics to be represented in the visual version, can be performed; furthermore, we can add **attributes** to the data (also called *metadata*) that may be used to logically organize the tabular data. The intermediate data structure, of the example we are processing, could therefore look like the following:

User	Read	Posted
Enzo	90	10
Giorgio	134	20
Luigi	89	3
Michele	14	0
Orazio	117	13

In this structure in particular, we have filtered out some information, such as the date and time of each logged event, as they are irrelevant to the current problem. The attributes *read* and *posted* are calculated from the data featured in the log file.

2.1.2 Visual Mapping

The key problems of this process lie in defining which visual structures to use to map the data and their location in the display area. As we have already mentioned, abstract data don't necessarily have a real location in physical space. There are some types of abstract data that, by their very nature, can easily find a spatial location. For example, the data taken from a monitoring station for atmospheric pollution can easily find a position on a geographic map, given that the monitoring stations that take the measurements are situated in a precise point in the territory. The same can be said for data taken from entities that have a topological structure, such as the traffic data of a computer network. However, there are several types of data that belong to entities that have no natural geographic or topological positioning. Think, for example, of the bibliographic references in scientific texts, of the consumption of car fuel, or of the salaries of various professional figures within a company. This type of data doesn't have an immediate correspondence with the dimensions of the physical space that surround it.

We must therefore define the visual structures that correspond to the data that we want to represent visually. This process is called *visual mapping*. Three structures must be defined [8]:

1. spatial substrate,
2. graphical elements,
3. graphical properties.

The **spatial substrate** defines the dimensions in physical space where the visual representation is created. The spatial substrate can be defined in terms of axes. In Cartesian space, the spatial substrate corresponds to x- and y-axes. Each axis can be of different types, depending on the type of data that we want to map on it. In particular, an axis can be *quantitative*, when there is a metric associated to the values reported on the axis; *ordinal*, when the values are reported on the axis in an order that corresponds to the order of the data; and *nominal,* when the region of an axis is divided into a collection of subregions without any intrinsic order.

The **graphical elements** are everything visible that appears in the space. There are four possible types of visual elements: points, lines, surfaces, and volumes (see Fig. 2.2).

The **graphical properties** are properties of the graphical elements to which the retina of the human eye is very sensitive (for this reason, they are also called *retinal variables*). They are independent of the position occupied by a visual element in spatial substrate. The most common graphical properties are size, orientation, color, texture, and shape. These are applied to the graphical elements and determine the properties of the visual layout that will be presented in the view (see Fig. 2.3).

In terms of human's visual perception, not all graphical properties behave in the same way. Some graphical properties are more effective than others from the viewpoint of quantitative values. Cleveland and McGill [11] carried out a study to evaluate the accuracy with which people are able to perceive quantitative values mapped to different properties, graphical elements, and spatial substrates. The study defined

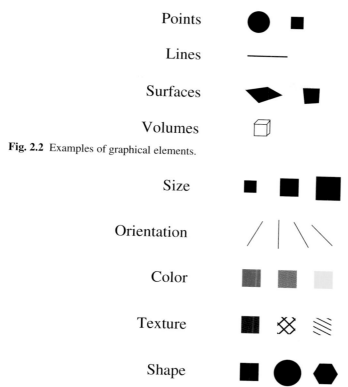

Points

Lines

Surfaces

Volumes

Fig. 2.2 Examples of graphical elements.

Size

Orientation

Color

Texture

Shape

Fig. 2.3 Examples of graphical properties.

a classification that is reported in Fig. 2.4, from which we can deduce that spatial positioning is one of the most accurate ways to perceive quantitative information. The chosen mapping has to make the most important conceptual attributes also become perceptively accurate.

Color has to be given particular attention. In fact, color is the only graphical property in which perception can depend on cultural, linguistic, and physiological factors. Some populations, for example, use a limited number of terms to define the entire color spectrum (in some populations, there are only two words to describe the colors: black and white). It is therefore possible that two people from different cultures may use diverse terminology to identify the same color or may even have different perceptions, given that they might not have a specific term for identifying a determined color on a cognitive level. Studies on perception [65] have demonstrated that, even taking the cultural differences into account, the colors that can be considered primary are white, black, red, green, yellow, and blue. These are the only colors that have the same name all over the world and, consequently, are the colors that must be chosen when it is necessary to map a category attribute to a maximum of six colors. Colin Ware [65] suggests limiting any mapping of categor-

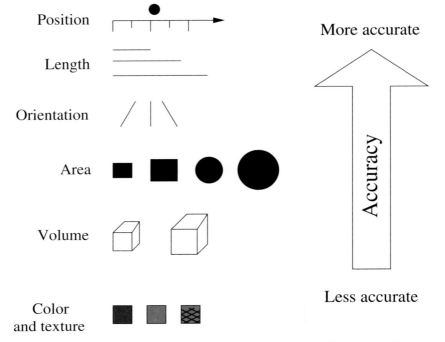

Fig. 2.4 Accuracy in the perception of quantitative values for some graphical and spatial elements.

ical attributes to these six primary colors, but, if necessary, it is possible to extend the list by adding pink, brown, cyan, orange, and purple. To represent quantitative attributes, or where there is an ordering of values, the use of primary colors is not advisable, because (1) there might not be enough primary colors, and (2) our culture does not adopt any convention on the ordering of colors (does blue come before or after yellow?). A clever idea might be to use a convention on a color scale, to be clearly explained in the application (from green to red, for example), or to vary the color intensity to codify the various levels of values (Fig. 2.5).

It is also necessary to bear in mind that a large percentage of the population (in Australia, 8% of males and 0.4% of females) has a particular ocular visual perception problems: *daltonism*.[1] People who suffer from this condition are generally unable to distinguish between red and green, or (less frequently) between yellow and blue. It is therefore important to consider that there are some people with this visual defect and to develop applications in which it is possible to change the color mapping.

Let's return to the example that we had been studying. To continue with the process of generation, we have to associate a visual structure with which to map the

---

[1] The term "daltonism" originates from the name of the English physicist John Dalton (1766–1844), who was the first to study this defect.

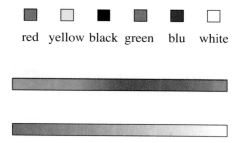

red   yellow black green   blu   white

Fig. 2.5 Use of primary colors to define categorical attributes (top) and color scales to define ordinal attributes (bottom).

data that we wish to represent, to the data structures. In the specified case, we have three attributes to represent:

Attribute	Data type
user	categorical
read	quantitative
posted	quantitative

We can resolve to map the attributes *read* and *posted* to the x- and y-coordinates on a Cartesian axis. Since it deals with quantitative data, the mapping can be carried out without any problems. This constitutes the **spatial substrate**. We then choose to represent each element individually in the spatial substrate with a point-type **graphical element**. The graphical element will be square-shaped and colored blue. In this way, we have defined the **graphical property** that will contain the element to be represented in the picture. We also decide to add a further graphical element, comprising a textual tag that contains the values of the attribute *user*, using the same spatial substrate as previously defined. We have therefore completed the visual mapping for all of the attributes in play.

2.1.3 Views

The views are the final result of the generation process. They are the result of the mapping of data structures to the visual structures, generating a visual representation in the physical space represented by the computer. They are what we see displayed on the computer screen. Figure 2.6 represents a possible view for the example we are dealing with.

The visual representation allows for efficient responses to the questions we posed on the analysis of discussions, recognizing who posts the most messages on the forum and who, on the other hand, reads messages without actively participating in

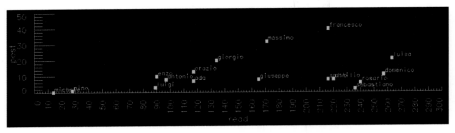

Fig. 2.6 A possible visual representation of the data collected from a discussion forum.

the discussions. In Fig. 2.6, we can identify the users *francesco* and *massimo*, who have been the most active both in posting new messages on the forum and also in reading. The users *rosario* and *sebastiano* have, instead, read many messages but have participated very little with their own messages. Finally, we can immediately single out the users *michele* and *nino*, who have been inactive in both reading and submitting new messages.

The views are characterized by a difficult inherent problem, a quantity of data to be represented that is too large for the available space. This is a problem that we come across rather frequently, given that very often real situations involve a very large amount of data (at times even millions of items). In these cases, when the display area is too small to visibly support all the elements of a visual representation, certain techniques are used, including zooming, panning, scrolling, focus + context, and magic lenses. These techniques will be discussed in more detail in Chapter 7.

2.2 Designing a Visual Application

A generation process, such as the one described previously, should be preceded by good design. Correct design is the key to the success of this type of application. Many prototypes developed in the context of scientific research don't even define what type of user the visualization model is addressing or the purpose of its development.

The main problem in designing a visual representation lies in creating visual mapping that, on the one hand, faithfully reproduces the information codified in the data and, on the other, facilitates the user in the predetermined goal. As we already discussed in Section 1.8, there is no way to know, given a collection of abstract data, which type of visual representation is suitable for such data. This depends on the nature of the data, the type of user it's designed for, the type of information that has to be represented, and its use, but also on the creativity, experience, and ability of the representation's designers. In these cases, the most precious and important information comes to us from potential users of the visual application, those who will use the system and ordain its success or failure. Believe it or not, most authors of works of visual representation of information don't carry out preliminary research with the users of the system to understand their actual needs, or only afterwards do they effectuate empirical evaluation, when the application prototype has been developed.

The procedure to follow, when creating the visual representations of abstract data, can be outlined in the following steps:

1. **Define the problem** by spending a certain amount of time with potential users of the visual representation. Identify their effective needs and how they work. This is needed to clearly define what has to be represented. Why is a representation needed? Is it needed to communicate something? Is it needed for finding new information? Or is it needed to prove hypotheses? It is necessary to bear in mind the human factors specific to the target audience that the application will address and, in particular, their cognitive and perceptive abilities. This will influence the choice of which visual models to use, to allow users to understand the information.

2. **Examine the nature of the data to represent**. The data can be *quantitative* (e.g., a list of integers or real numbers), *ordinal* (data of a non numeric nature, but which have their own intrinsic order, such as the days of the week), or *categorical* (data that have no intrinsic order, such as the names of people or cities). A different mapping may be appropriate, according to the data type.

3. **Number of dimensions**. The number of dimensions of the data (also called *attributes*) that we need to represent very importantly determines the type of representation that we use. The attributes can be *independent* or *dependent*. The dependent attributes are those that vary and whose behavior we are interested in analyzing with respect to the independent attributes. According to the number of dependent attributes, we have a collection of data that is called *univariate* (one dimension varies with respect to another), *bivariate* (there are two dependent dimensions), *trivariate* (three dependent dimensions), or *multivariate* (four or more dimensions that vary compared to the independent ones).

4. **Data structures**. These can be *linear* (the data are codified in linear data structures like vectors, tables, collections, etc.), *temporal* (data that change in time), *spatial* or *geographical* (data that have a correspondence with something physical, such as a map, floorplan, etc.), *hierarchical* (data relative to entities organized on hierarchy, for example, genealogy, flowcharts, files on a disk, etc.), and *network* (data that describe relationships between entities).

5. **Type of interaction**. This determines if the visual representation is *static* (e.g., an image printed on paper or an image represented on a computer screen but not modifiable by the user), *transformable* (when the user can control the process of modification and transformation of data, such as varying some parameters of data entry, varying the extremes of the values of some attributes, or choosing a different mapping for view creation), or *manipulable* (the user can control and modify some parameters that regulate the generation of the views, like zooming on a detail or rotating an image represented in 3D). The model represented in Fig. 2.1 illustrates at which levels of the process these types of interactions come into play.

The elements just described, to be considered during the design stage, are summarized in Table 2.1.

Problem	Data type	Dimensions	Data structure	Type of interaction
Communicate	Quantitative	Univariate	Linear	Static
Explore	Ordinal	Bivariate	Temporal	Transformable
Confirm	Categorical	Trivariate	Spatial	Manipulable
		Multivariate	Hierarchical	
			Network	

Table 2.1 Variables to consider when designing visual representations.

Each of the possible options described here can point to the use of a specific technique. Furthermore, correct design should also define suitable tools for assessing the effects of the proposed representations on the users' performance. Evaluation is discussed in Chapter 8. In the following sections, we will illustrate the most common types of representation, keeping in mind the most distinctive aspect, which is the number of dimensions. We'll start by looking at linear data. Other data organizations (spatial, hierarchical, and network structures) will be discussed in next chapters.

2.3 Visual Representation of Linear Data

A collection of data is defined as **univariate** when one of its attributes varies with respect to one or more independent attributes. Let's suppose that we have to analyze the gross national product (GNP) realized by some nations in 2000. A tabular version, as shown in Table 2.2, is the most efficient form for immediately identifying the GNP of one of the featured nations. Basically, a specific nation and its corresponding GNP can be singled out immediately from the alphabetically ranked list. It may be interesting, however, to compare the GNP of one nation with that of another. For this particular task, the tabular version featured here is not the ideal solution, and it is better to explore other types of representation.

One possible graphical form is the *single-axis scatterplot* (Fig. 2.7 on the left). It consists of representing a single-axis spatial substrate and positioning a visual element according to the value of the dependent attribute, which in this case is represented by a circular shape to which a label is also attached. We can immediately make out which nations have the highest and lowest GNP, while some groupings are clear. For example, it is instantly noticeable how the GNP of Brazil and Spain differ very little, while Germany has a notably higher GNP than the following nation, France.

Nation	GNP
Argentina	284.2
Brazil	601.7
Canada	713.8
France	1308.4
Germany	1870.2
Italy	1074.8
New Zealand	52.2
Poland	166.5
Portugal	106.5
Spain	561.8
Switzerland	246.2
The Netherlands	370.6

Table 2.2 Gross national product (GNP) of some nations in 2000. Values expressed in billions of USD. Source: The World Bank, *World Development Indicators 2005*.

Another very common form of univariate representation is the bar chart. The data in Table 2.2 can also be represented using the bar chart shown in Fig. 2.7 on the right. Scatterplots and bar charts are two relatively common forms of visual representation of information. Their popularity is due to the fact that they deal with two very simple shapes, immediately clear and understandable. Through the scatterplot, we are able to instantly take in the global distribution of GNP all along the values axis, while the bar chart allows us to make very efficient comparisons between the different nations. On the other hand, only in very rare cases are the data that need to be

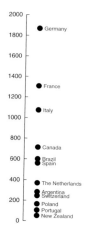
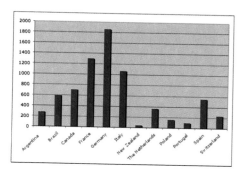

Fig. 2.7 The GNP of various nations visually represented by a single-axis scatterplot (left) and a bar chart (right).

Nation	Export	Import
Argentina	10.9	11.5
Brazil	10.7	12.2
Canada	46.1	40.3
France	28.5	27.3
Germany	33.8	33.4
Italy	28.3	27.3
New Zealand	35.9	34.2
Poland	27.8	34.4
Portugal	31.5	42.8
Spain	30.1	32.4
Switzerland	45.6	39.9
The Netherlands	67.5	62.2

Table 2.3 Total import and export values of some nations in 2000. Values expressed in percentages of the GNP. Source: The World Bank, *World Development Indicators 2005*.

analyzed univariate, and so we are concerned with analyzing the cases in which the number of dependent attributes is greater than one.

When the number of dependent attributes is two, we speak of **bivariate** data representation. Let's suppose that we need to examine the total value of the overseas import and exports goods of these nations. In this case also, the values can be reported in a table (see Table 2.3). However, to have an effective vision of the import and export distribution of these nations, we can represent these values on a two-axis scatterplot (Fig. 2.8).

This type of representation has very high expressive power, given that the most important data (import and export) are mapped onto the axes and, as we have seen in Section 2.1.2, they are the most accurate visual way to perceive quantitative infor-

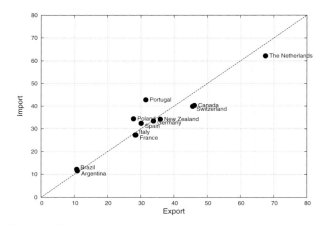

Fig. 2.8 Two-dimensional scatterplot that compares import and export values.

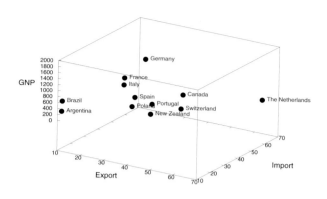

Fig. 2.9 A three-dimensional scatterplot.

mation. In the picture, the median line is indicated, leading us to immediately notice how the nations of Portugal, Poland, Spain, Brazil, and Argentina had a much higher import-based economy in 2000.

The term **trivariate** representation is used when three dependent attributes vary with respect to one or more independent attributes. This case becomes complicated, since the two spatial dimensions we have used until now to map the dependent attributes are not sufficient. Because we live in a three-dimensional world, we are well used to observing objects represented in three-dimensional spaces. Therefore, a very natural thing to do is to extend a scatterplot to include a third dimension, which we represent through perspective. Figure 2.9 provides us with an example of a scatterplot in which we have grouped the GNP and import and export values of the previously featured nations.

Representations like Fig. 2.9 typically present two types of problems. First of all, in three-dimensional (3D) representations, *occlusion* problems can occur, meaning there is a possibility that some graphical elements are "hidden" behind the elements in front. Second, it is difficult to identify the position of the graphical elements with respect to the axes. For instance, in Fig. 2.9, it is very difficult to understand whether France or Canada has a higher import value.

There are various strategies for solving these types of problems, which are intrinsic to all 3D representations, such as rotating the image to reveal the occluded objects or identify the values associated with each axis. Another solution could be using a two-dimensional scatterplot and mapping an attribute using other graphical properties, like color or the dimension of the graphical elements. For example, in Fig. 2.10 the third attribute is mapped to the area of the graphical elements or to a color scale. In this way, the third dimension is sacrificed, but, on the other hand, we have a clearer and more precise visual representation. Nevertheless, the occlusion problem still remains.

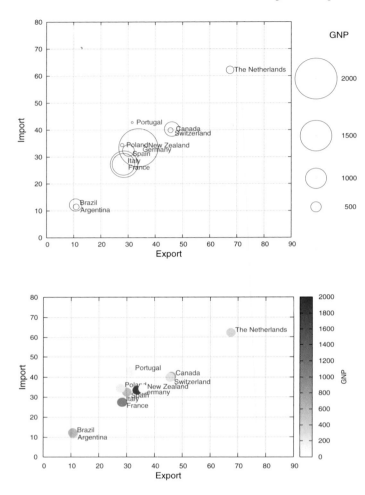

Fig. 2.10 A two-dimensional scatterplot with GNP mapped by the area of the circle (top image) and by a color scale (bottom image).

2.4 2D vs. 3D

In the previous section we looked at a situation in which a collection of trivariate data is represented by two-and three-dimensional spatial views. We have also demonstrated how 2D representations are clearer and more precise than 3D, due to some intrinsic problems that afflict the 3D views. However, we are used to representing the images on a two-dimensional screen, so that the third dimension is simulated by using perspective. Furthermore, some empirical studies have shown that 3D representations increase *cognitive load*, or the user's mental effort to cor-

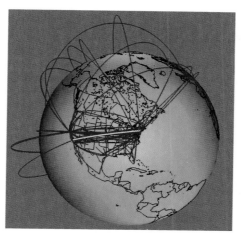

Fig. 2.11 Graphic representation of the topology of the Internet network MBone on a terrestrial scale. Image reproduced with the permission of Tamara Munzner and © 1996 IEEE.

rectly interpret the data represented. Does this mean that 3D representations are to be avoided in any case? Not always.

As a general rule, we can say that 2D representations should be preferred over 3D. 3D representations are to be used in limited and particular cases. One case in which 3D representation works wonderfully is, for example, when there is a need to represent an object in movement, or when the data to be represented have a three-dimensional spatial component, like the Earth or the structure of a molecule. Figure 2.11 visually represents the topology of the data transmission network used by the Internet in multicast modality (MBone, *multicast backbone*) [45]. The image is represented through VRML technology, which allows a user to visualize and explore the globe interactively to understand the structure of this network's topology in every part of the planet. Certainly, this is a very effective representation of a table of Internet IP addresses and numbers. Thanks to the usage of VRML technology, the interactivity allows the best use of this 3D representation.

2.5 Conclusion

In this chapter, we have presented a reference model that describes the procedure that generates interactive visual representations from data, by means of a pipeline of three stages: preprocessing and data transformations, visual mapping, and view creation. Each of these was analyzed in detail with a practical example. We saw how some operations, such as the choice of graphical elements and properties to be used in the visual mapping stage, are crucial and depend on the experience and ability of the system's designer. We suggested a procedure to follow when designing visual applications. Finally, we introduced some examples of visual representations for univariate, bivariate, and trivariate data.

Chapter 3
Perception

In the previous chapter, we saw how visual mapping is the most critical aspect in designing a visual representation. Views generated by these processes create strong visual representation of data because the elements we use to encode this data (lines, points, shapes, color, etc.) are processed by visual perception rapidly and efficiently. Mapping data attributes to proper graphical elements and properties is paramount to creating effective visual representation of data. The designer of such systems has to have a sound knowledge of how the different types of visual attributes are perceived by human vision. In a visual representation that aims to discover patterns in data, if the attributes are mapped in a certain way, the patterns are easily perceivable, while they become invisible when mapped in other ways. The "trick" is to visually represent data in such a way that the most important patterns are encoded with "popping-out" visual forms, clearly distinguishable from their surroundings. Due to the importance of mapping data effectively, this chapter contains the principles of visual perception with practical indications.

3.1 Memory

The term "memory" has slightly different meanings when used in different contexts. In computers, the memory is the part of hardware dedicated to storing data and can be accessed upon request. Data are encoded in binary values and are processed by the central processing unit (CPU) by means of programs; hence, in computers, there is a clear distinction among data, process, and programs. In organisms, the memory is a function of the brain, which is not only able to store information, but also to process and reason, and it constitutes the common ground for perception, categorization, interpretation, thinking, etc., all in the same organ (although certain activities are localized in specific areas of the brain). In fact, we receive light through the eye, which generates a visual stimulus. This stimulus is translated into neural signals by the retina and passed to the brain, where it is processed and perceived.

R. Mazza, *Introduction to Information Visualization*,
DOI: 10.1007/978-1-84800-219-7_3, © Springer-Verlag London Limited 2009

Hence, it is in the brain that we perceive the images, make sense of them, and store our memories.

Cognitive psychology identifies several types of memories. With the aim of understanding how visual representation is perceived and stored in memory, it is worth mentioning the following types of memory, based on the duration of memory retention:

- **Sensory memory** is the ability of the brain to retain impressions of signals coming from sensor organs for a very short period of time, between 250 and 500 milliseconds or less. Visual sensory memory is more commonly referred to as *iconic memory*. This type of memory is able to store visual information from the eyes, independent of conscious control, and automatically. For this reason, the processing that takes place in iconic memory is called *preattentive processing*, as it is processed without the need for focused attention [57]. During preattentive processing, only a limited set of visual attributes is detected. Such basic features include colors, closure, line ends, contrast, tilt, curvature, and size [57].
- Some of the information in sensory memory is then transferred to **short-term memory**, where it remains from a few seconds to a minute (without rehearsal). If it is periodically rehearsed, it can remain for a few hours. This memory has limited storage capacity (some experiments showed that the store of short-term memory is between five and nine equally weighted items [44]), is conscious, and involves an attentive process of perception. The capacity of the short-term memory can be increased when information is organized in *chunks*, such as when we memorize phone numbers: By memorizing a number as several chunks of two or three numbers, it is easier to remember than when we try to memorize it as a simple sequence of digits. In visual representations, an example of a chunk of information is when, in a bar chart, we encode a categorical attribute with bars of different colors. A chunk of information (for instance, the information encoded with blue-colored bars) can be kept in the viewer's short-memory very efficiently. It is important, however, not to provide an excessive number of chunks that the viewer has to retain in memory.
- Information in short-term memory is easily forgotten after a brief period of time unless we rehearse it periodically or make meaningful associations. This type of memory can store information for many years, even for life, and is called **long-term memory**. Short-term memories became long-term by reinforcing the structure of neuronal synapses through a process called *long-term potentiation*.

The properties of sensory, short-term, and long-term memory have important implications in the design of a visual representation. In particular, preattentive visual processing, which takes place in the sensory memory, is fundamental for creating visual representations, as preattentive visual attributes are perceived by the reader almost instantaneously, without the intervention of consciousness. These attributes "pop out" from their surroundings [65]; therefore, most important data attributes, or items that have to be represented together as a group, should be encoded with preattentive attributes. These attributes will be described in detail later in this chapter.

In visual representations, mapping information is usually retained in the short-term memory. Since this type of memory has limited capacity and holds information for a few seconds, designers of visual representations shouldn't constrain users to remember more than nine chunks of information. For instance, if you design a chart that maps different data types with different shapes, there should not be more than nine data types (although less than five is ideal), and you should avoid splitting a representation into multiple windows (or request the user to scroll through the window), because if the image is no longer visible, the user has to retain a large quantity of data in short-term memory.

3.2 Preattentive Properties

Thanks to some studies in psychology, a number of visual properties that are preattentively processed have been identified [57]. According to Colin Ware [65], these can be grouped into four basic categories: *color*, *form*, *movement*, and *spatial position*. We will look at them in the following paragraphs.

3.2.1 Color

Colors can be expressed in different mathematical models. One of these is the *HSL* color system, which stands for *hue*, *saturation*, and *lightness*. Each color can be described by the composition of these three elements. In particular, the hue is the aspect of a color that we describe with names such "red," "green," etc. Saturation and lightness are related concepts that refer to the intensity of a specific color.

Hue and intensity are processed preattentively and work very well in the visual detection of elements that are distinguished from the surroundings, without the need for a sequential search, as in Fig. 3.1, where the letter C "pops out" from others because of the use of a preattentive attribute of hue (top) and intensity (bottom).

3.2.2 Form

Preattentive attributes of form are listed in Table 3.1, together with an example. Examples of preattentive attributes of form are also depicted in Fig. 3.2.

3.2.3 Spatial Position

The following are preattentive attributes of spatial position:

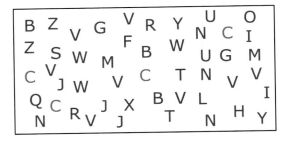

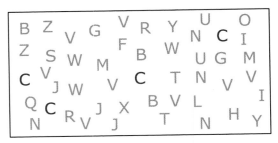

Fig. 3.1 Example showing how the hue and intensity of colors are processed preattentively, resulting in a quick distinction of elements.

- **2D position**, as we have seen in Fig. 2.4, is the most accurate attribute for encoding quantitative data in graphs.
- **Stereoscopic depth** is the result of the combination of the images received by both eyes. Thanks to the difference in the image location of an object seen by the left and right eyes (called *binocular disparity*), human eyes are able to preat-

Attribute	Example
Orientation	A line with a different orientation than the others
Length	The length of bars in a bar chart, as we have seen in Fig. 1.2
Width	The width of the line that we use to highlight parts of a figure
Size	The size of a shape, to rank a particular data attribute
Collinearity	Lines that follow the same direction
Curvature	Lines and object borders can be straight or curved
Spatial grouping	Groups of objects, such as a cluster
Added marks	Adding a mark in a set of objects to highlight one in particular
Shape	A square in a group of circles
Numerosity	Cardinality in groups of objects

Table 3.1 Preattentive attributes of form.

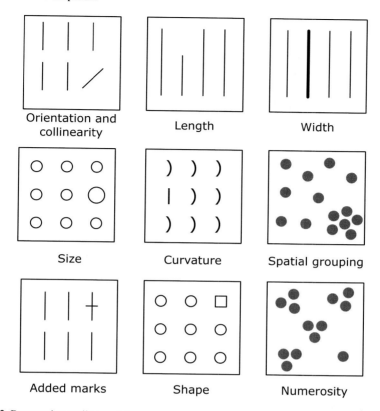

Fig. 3.2 Preattentive attributes of form.

tentively perceive depth. Stereoscopic vision can be reproduced by a computer using two different cameras.

- **Concavity/convexity** is produced in images through the effect of shading, such as the example given in Fig. 3.3.

Fig. 3.3 Preattentive attributes of concavity/convexity.

3.2.4 Movement

Attributes of movement are **flicker** and **motion**. These are the most effective ways to get our attention. Often abused in websites (fickering advertisements are always annoying), they are used in dashboards as powerful attention-getters in situations that require immediate user intervention.

3.3 Mapping Data to Preattentive Attributes

The designer of a visual application has to carefully consider the attributes to be mapped into the visual presentation and decide which graphical property to use for each data attribute. This process is called visual mapping and has already been discussed in Section 2.1.2. In the light of what we have seen in this chapter, it is clear how visual preattentive attributes are very powerful, as they are immediately perceived without the need for conscious attention. Colin Ware describes these visual attributes as "the most important contribution that vision science can make to data visualization" [65]. However, this mapping cannot be done automatically, as the number of preattentive attributes that can be used in a single representation, and the number of visual distinctions of a single attribute, are limited. These limitations are due to our short-term memory feature that has to process the meaning of each encoding.

For instance, we can use distinct shapes or hues to represent census data in different years. This can work if the number of years is limited; if the number of years is very large, the encoding becomes inefficient, as readers are only able to distinguish a limited number of shapes or hues. Ware [65] suggests limiting to no more than eight different hues, four different orientations, four different sizes, and all the other visual preattentive attributes to less than 10 distinct values. Few [19] instead chooses a more prudent approach and suggests limiting the number of distinctions, for any attribute, to no more than four.

A similar limitation exists on the number of visual attributes that we adopt in a representation. Also, the combination of particular preattentive attributes cannot usually be detected preattentively. Let's look at the latter case with an example, illustrated in Fig. 3.4. The identification of gray squares is very slow, as the combination of gray-colored objects and square-shaped objects is not preattentive: We are forced to do a serial scan to locate the gray squares.

Now the point is: I have a dataset with a particular attribute to represent. Which preattentive attribute should I choose for it? We have already seen in Fig. 2.4 that Cleveland and McGill empirically verified that some attributes are more accurate than others for judging quantitative values. But we may also have categorical and ordinal types of attributes. Some scientists have addressed the issue of finding a mapping between data types and preattentive attributes. One of them, Mackinlay [39], even proposed a ranking of the accuracy of perceptual tasks that can be defined when encoding quantitative, ordinal, and categorical data with different graphical el-

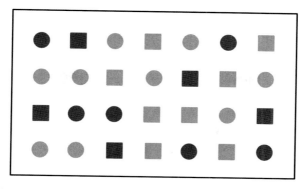

Fig. 3.4 Combinations of more preattentive attributes (in the image, lightness and shape) may prevent the preattentive identification of an object.

ements and properties. But recent studies have shown that things are more complex than they appear, and many factors influence the choice of encoding [55]. Therefore, a universal, generic, ranking of preattentive attributes does not exist. However, it does not mean that an indicative rule of thumb cannot be arranged. Some preattentive attributes work better with quantitative data types, while others are more effective with categorical or ordinal data types. Table 3.2 (inspired by a work by Stephen Few [19] and extended with the ordinal and categorical data types) can help in this.

3.4 Postattentive Processing

When we look at a bar chart, such as the one depicted in Fig. 2.7, we can immediately perceive the different lengths of the bars. As we have seen, this process is performed preattentively. Then we must turn our attention to the text on the horizontal axis to detect which country corresponds to the longest (or shortest) bar. Now we can leave the chart and look at something else (for instance, the single-axis scatterplot on the left). What happens when the attention is taken away from the bar chart, concentrates on something else, and then focuses on the chart once again? Does the viewer gain a richer understanding of the bar chart when the attention is applied to the chart the second time?

This aspect, called *postattentive processing*, was studied by Wolfe et al. [68]. They ran some experiments and found that attention has no cumulative effects on visual perception. In other words, if a viewer looks at one scene numerous times and then looks at something else, the new preattentive representation (or postattentive representation) of an object appears to be identical to its representation before the viewer focused his attention on it. The preattentive visual perception doesn't save any information about the scene. The viewer may know more about an ob-

Attribute	Quantitative	Ordinal	Categorical
Color			
Hue	×	×	✓
Intensity	−	✓	×
Form			
Orientation	−	−	×
Length	✓	−	×
Width	−	−	×
Size	−	−	×
Collinearity	×	×	×
Curvature	−	−	×
Spatial grouping	×	×	×
Added marks	×	×	✓
Shape	×	×	✓
Numerosity	✓	✓	×
Spatial position			
2D position	✓	✓	−
Stereoscopic depth	×	×	×
Concavity/convexity	−	−	×
Movement			
Flicker	×	×	−
Motion	−	−	×

Table 3.2 Encoding quantitative, ordinal, and categorical data with different preattentive attributes. ✓ indicates that the attribute is suitable for the data type. − indicates a limited suitability. × indicates that the attribute does not work well with that data type.

served object after focusing on it again, but that knowledge does not alter the visual representation that the viewer has, in his mind, of that object.

This result has important implications on how visual representations are perceived. In particular, previewing a scene or paying prolonged attention to the objects does not make a visual search more efficient. Each object is recognized individually. Even if we study a display, we must apply the same preattentive effort to locating a particular object in a new, different scene. We cannot teach or improve viewers' preattentive capabilities.

3.5 Gestalt Principles

When we look at a image, such as the one depicted in Fig. 3.5, we can easily recognize that it represents a little house. But if we observe it in more detail, we can see how this image is a simple composition of a triangle and three rectangles that, arranged as in Fig. 3.5, lets us perceive an image portraying a little house rather than four simple geometric elements.

Fig. 3.5 A composition of simple geometric elements (triangle and rectangles) is perceived as a little house.

This phenomenon was studied by Gestalt theorists (in particular, Max Wertheimer [66], Wolfgang Köhler [35], and Kurt Koffka [34]) starting in 1920, who determined innate mental laws by which objects were perceived. Gestalt's basic principle is that the whole (the picture of the house) is not the simple sum of its parts (the triangle and rectangles) but has a greater meaning than its individual components. Gestalt principles aim to define the rules according to which human perception tends to organize visual elements into a "unified whole," also referred to as groups (from which the German term *gestalt* derives.) They are still valid today and can offer interesting insights into the design of visual representations. These principles are discussed next.

3.5.1 Figure and Ground

The figure and ground principle states that our perception tends to separate an object from its background, based on visual attributes, such as contrast, color, size, etc. A simple case is represented in Fig. 3.5. In this case, the image is perceived as being articulated into two components: the figure (the little house) and the ground (the black background).

3.5.2 Proximity

The proximity principle states that when elements are placed close together, they tend to be perceived as forming a group. See, for instance, Fig. 3.6. In the image to the left, squares are placed without proximity and so are perceived as 12 separate elements. In the central image, we see squares forming four groups. Even if the shapes or colors of the objects are different, they will appear as a group, as can be seen in the image on the right.

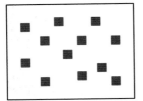 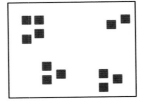 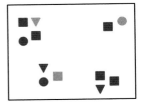

Fig. 3.6 Gestalt proximity example: Objects are perceived as separate elements (left) or as groups (center and right).

3.5.3 Similarity

The similarity principle states that objects with similar shape, size, color, orientation, and texture are perceived as belonging together, forming a group. In Fig. 3.7 on the left, objects of two distinct sizes seem to belong to the same group. Also, in the figure on the right, the filled and empty squares are associated naturally and we tend to see alternating rows of filled and empty squares.

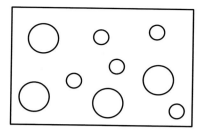 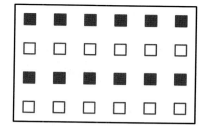

Fig. 3.7 Gestalt similarity example: Objects of the same size (on left) or different color (on right) are perceived as belonging to the same group.

3.5.4 Closure

The closure principle states that when an object is not complete, or the space is not completely enclosed, and enough elements are present, then the parts tend to be grouped together and we perceive the whole figure. See examples in Fig. 3.8.

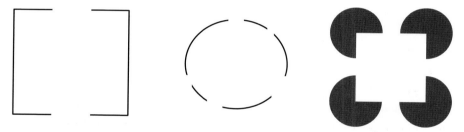

Fig. 3.8 Gestalt closure example: We tend to see complete figures even when part of the information is missing (left and center images) or when elements are aligned in such a way that the viewer perceives them as connected (right image).

3.5.5 Continuity

The continuity principle states that if an object appears to form a continuation of another object, beyond the ending points, we perceive the pieces as parts of a whole object. Some examples are depicted in Fig. 3.9. On the left, we see two triangles interrupted by a horizontal line; we don't see (although it could be another possible interpretation of the image) two small triangles laid on the line, and two trapezoids below. The same in the center and right images: We perceive an X sign (not four joint lines forming two symmetric corners), and the viewer's eye naturally follows the curved line, although it is interrupted and joined to another segment.

Fig. 3.9 Gestalt continuity example: Human mind naturally follow a line or a curve.

3.5.6 Other Principles

The Gestalt principles described above are the classics mentioned in literature, but there are several others, less common, that are not illustrated here. There is no definitive list of Gestalt principles, but we can mention the **common region principle** (objects enclosed by a boundary are perceived as a group), **connection principle** (objects that are connected are perceived as a group), and **symmetry principle** (symmetrical images are perceived as a group).

3.6 Conclusion

In this chapter, we have described the most important principles of visual perception. We have seen how short-term memory and preattentive processing play an extremely important role in the design of effective visual representations, where the most important information can "pop out" from the surroundings through the mapping of data with preattentive attributes. Also, the designer of visual representations can take advantage of the basic Gestalt principles, as they can offer interesting insights into the design of groups of elements.

Chapter 4
Multivariate Analysis

We have already introduced the concept of multivariate data, which are collections of data in which many attributes (usually more than four) change with respect to one or more independent attributes. We find numerous examples in the activities that we carry out every day. Take, for instance, the act of entering a shop to buy a cellular phone. We are normally greeted by an overwhelming number of models, all offering the most diverse features. Frequency bands, Bluetooth, camera, GPRS, MMS, WAP, speakerphone, and even Wi-Fi are just some of the numerous modern features that often influence our choice of one cell phone over another. To decide which cell phone to buy, we take the features that interest us the most into consideration and, from the various models, we choose the phone that most satisfies our requirements. Since there are many models, with features that evolve every six months in any case, very often we turn to the sales assistants to help us in the difficult task of choosing the cell phone that's right for us.

This is an example in which a decision process (the purchase of goods), based on a collection of multidimensional data (the technical features of the phones), is aided by an external agent (the sales assistant) with experience in and knowledge of the goods that we wish to purchase. This process works excellently when the number of instances (cell phones) and attributes (features) is fairly contained. What would happen if the number of cell phones were extremely large, let's say a hundred or even a thousand? Would the salesperson manage to cope with all of this data and advise us on the right phone without the aid of supplementary tools?

It's not by mere chance that one of the sectors in which information visualization is enjoying great success are the decision support systems, which are a specific class of software systems that help in decision-making activities. These systems are characterized by a great amount of data and numerous attributes and are very important as they provide essential information for managers, analysts, and directors, who are required to make decisions that are crucial for the running of the company.

In this chapter, we will analyze some of the most common techniques of the visual representation of multivariate data. We will also show some successful cases and examples of representations for the explorative analysis of large quantities of multivariate data.

R. Mazza, *Introduction to Information Visualization*,
DOI: 10.1007/978-1-84800-219-7_4, © Springer-Verlag London Limited 2009

4.1 The Problem of Multivariate Visualization

In Chapter 2, we looked at some examples of bivariate and trivariate data, represented simply by a scatterplot on Cartesian axes. Scatterplots are very simple and intuitive visual forms and work well when there are two dependent attributes. Their values are mapped along the values of the Cartesian axes. However, the number of situations in which one or two dependent attributes are involved is very limited, and most real problems have a rather high number of dependent attributes to analyze.

Scatterplots can be extended, allowing the mapping of more than two attributes. We can, for example, extend the scatterplots by adding further visual elements on which data mapping can be carried out (like shape, dimension, color, and texture), or adding a third dimension, represented by the perspective of the picture.

Working with these types of extensions, scatterplots can visually represent data in which up to seven different attributes can vary. Figure 4.1 is an example of a scatterplot that shows data from 174 countries and aims to compare the level of wealth (represented by the gross national income of each inhabitant) and the state of health of the resident population (represented by the number of deaths in children under five years old for every 1,000 births). These values are respectively mapped onto the x-axis and y-axis. Furthermore, they seek to report the number of inhabitants (mapped to the dimension of the graphical elements) and the continent to which each nation belongs (mapped to the color of the graphical element). One immediately notices an almost linear correlation between the wealth and the state of health: The state of health improves with an increase in the wealth in the population. There are also isolated cases that go against the grain with respect to the general trend; the most evident is represented by Cuba, whose population has an excellent level of health (even higher than that of the United States!), despite the wealth as being comparable to that of India. Other interesting information is drawn from the color of the circles. For example, the African nations are almost all grouped in the lower left-hand corner of the graph, indicating the state of extreme poverty and the terrible health levels in these unfortunate nations.

The scatterplot in Fig. 4.1 effectively highlights the relationship among wealth, state of health, number of inhabitants, and the continent to which each nation belongs. It is worth remembering, however, that the scatterplots are not suitable for all types of problems and data. If we wish to add other factors, such as the number of working hours per year, the average rent of an 80-square-meter apartment in the center of the capital, the cost of 1Kg. of bread, the number of paid holidays per year, etc., the scatterplot is no longer appropriate and so it's necessary to find appropriate forms of visualization. In the following sections, we will illustrate visualization techniques for multivariate data, grouping them as geometric, iconic, and pixel-based.

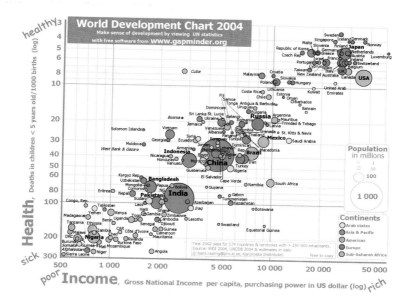

Fig. 4.1 Scatterplot representing four-variate attributes. Image published on the website http://www.gapminder.org on data derived from the United Nations statistical studies, with copy permission.

4.2 Geometric Techniques

Geometric techniques in information visualization consist of mapping the data of the attributes on a geometric space. Scatterplots belong to this category but are, unfortunately, limited by the fact that they have only two Cartesian axes on which to map two dimensions. In 1981, Alfred Inselberg, a researcher at IBM, had the brilliant idea of defining a geometric space through an arbitrary number of axes, arranging them parallely, instead of perpendicularly, as had been done in the Cartesian diagrams [28]. This was the origin of one of today's most common technique of visual representation of multivariate data.

4.2.1 Parallel Coordinates

This technique takes its name from the method with which the values of the attributes are represented: Every attribute corresponds to an axis and the axes are arranged to be parallel and equally spaced. Each record of the dataset is represented by a polygonal chain that connects the values of the attributes on its axes.

We'll look at an example to help us understand exactly how this type of representation works. Let's suppose that we have to represent the following data through parallel coordinates.

	Age	Weight	Sex
Vincenzo	32	75	M
Piero	24	63	M
Luisa	28	60	F
Giulia	18	58	F

Each record of the dataset has a different color to facilitate understanding of the generation process. It deals with trivariate data, two of which are numbers (age and weight) and one is categorical (sex). The name of the person is considered independent data. We represent these data by mapping values onto three parallel exes, using a quantitative spatial substrate for the first two attributes and nominal for the last (see Section 2.1.2). By joining the points corresponding to the coordinates of each record, we achieve the representation shown in Fig. 4.2.

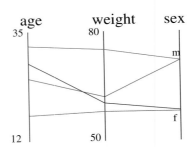

Fig. 4.2 Parallel coordinates representation.

We will now analyze a concrete case, using a dataset provided by *Xmdvtool* software, developed by Matthew Ward at Worcester Polytechnic in 1994, as an example [64]. The software is public domain and can be freely downloaded from the website.[1] The dataset provided contains the technical specifications of 392 car models produced in the 1970s, with seven dependent attributes. By analyzing the dataset using Xmdvtool software, we attain the visual representation illustrated in Fig. 4.3.

Parallel coordinates are a very powerful tool for the explorative analysis of data. For example, an inverse relationship between fuel consumption (MPG) and the number of cylinders in an automobile is easily discernable: The intersection of the lines that join the values between the two axes clearly demonstrates how the cars with a

---

[1] http://davis.wpi.edu/ xmdv/

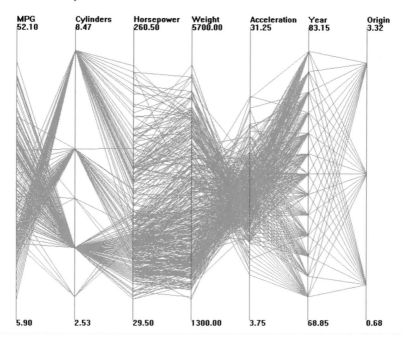

Fig. 4.3 Parallel coordinates for 730 elements with 7 variant attributes. Picture generated by Xmdvtool software.

high number of cylinders (in the upper part of the axes) cover fewer miles per gallon than those of fewer cylinders. Another clear inverse relationship is that between the weight of the automobile and acceleration: The heavier automobiles usually have a shorter acceleration (meaning the time necessary to reach a certain speed starting from standstill).

Although they are a very powerful tool of explorative analysis, parallel coordinates can present some problems with very large datasets (for instance, in datasets with 5,000 elements). In such cases, the visual representation could be too dense to distinguish the lines, reducing the representation to a single polygon of uniform color. This problem is intrinsic to any visual representation: The space available on the screen may be insufficient to contain all the visual elements. Also, the arrangement of the axes in the parallel coordinates is decisive for the analysis of the dependence between the various attributes. In particular, the dependence between the attributes represented by the immediately adjacent axes is obvious, while a direct analysis between attributes represented by distant axes might not be possible (for example, in Fig. 4.3, the correlation between the acceleration and MPG of the automobile is not immediately noticeable).

It is possible to intervene by means of interaction. First, the software enables the reordering of the axes. If we want to study the direct correlation between two attributes, we move the axes so that they are positioned one beside the other.

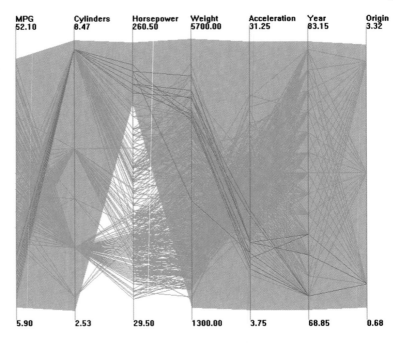

Fig. 4.4 Brushing of the values on the coordinate parallel axes. The red lines represent the elements that satisfy all of the limits on the values denoted by the violet polygon. Image generated by Xmdvtool software.

Another procedure that can be carried out on the parallel coordinates graph is the *brushing* of values of one or more attributes. In Fig. 4.4, the purple polygon selects, for each axis, the values on which the brushing is to be carried out. The red-colored lines mark the elements on which values fall on these intervals. By placing the cursor over an axis, one can read the corresponding value. Brushing can be very useful for carrying out explorative analysis of values. In Fig. 4.4, for example, we have brushed the automobiles that have less than 200 horsepower. Through brushing, we can deduce that all of the automobiles with this characteristic have 8 cylinders, were manufactured in the same country and, curiously, were all produced before 1973.

4.2.2 Scatterplot Matrix

Scatterplot matrices represent an interesting extension to the common 2D scatter-plot, to simply and intuitively represent a generic number of multivariate attributes. This very simple technique consists of representing pairs of attributes, through bidimensional scatterplots, and putting the scatterplots side by side to share the same

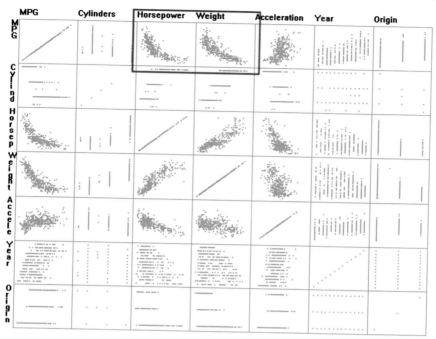

Fig. 4.5 Scatterplot matrices present multivariate data very simply and intuitively. Image generated by Xmdvtool software.

axes. In this way, an $N \times N$ matrix is formed, where N is the number of attributes to represent. Figure 4.5 illustrates an example, generated through Xmdvtool software, using the same dataset that was previously used for the parallel coordinates.

From the figure, the type of correlation that runs between the pairs of attributes can immediately be drawn. For example, it is very clear that, by increasing the horsepower and weight, the number of miles covered (in terms of miles per gallon, MPG) diminishes dramatically (see graphs included in the blue frame). We would also have been able to reach the same result through parallel coordinates, but, to analyze the various dependence between the pairs of attributes, we would have had to move the axes or perform brushing. Using the scatterplot matrices, however, makes the correlation between the pairs immediately visible, without needing to adjust the visual representation. On the other hand, the scatterplot matrices can present some inconveniences. In particular, for N attributes, it is necessary to form an $N \times N$ scatterplot matrix; therefore, the space available to represent the points is very limited. It is impossible to put labels to indicate the individual points, or select a particular point with the mouse to read the value of its coordinate. Moreover, the collective vision of all the attributes that we have observed in the scatterplot in Fig. 4.1 is lost when the scatterplot matrix is used.

4.2.3 TableLens

Spreadsheet applications, like Microsoft Excel, have become one of the most widespread types of software. Thanks to a very intuitive visual interface (but also thanks to some very effective marketing initiatives), this type of tool is part of the software equipment of every computer in use in a professional or domestic environment. The great intuition that the creators of this software had in the early 1980s was to use a structure similar to multiplication tables to perform the calculations, a very simple data organization that we have been used to since our early school years.[2] Following this principle, in 1994 John Lamping and Ramana Rao proposed a visual analysis tool for data called *TableLens* [48]. Its structure was inspired by spreadsheet applications, but its characteristic is to represent data using horizontal bars rather than numeric values. In particular, data are represented on a matrix, where attributes are represented on columns and every instance of data is reported on a row of the matrix. The numerical values of an attribute of the dataset are mapped to the length of horizontal bars. Visually, the horizontal bars can be represented in a very limited space. This way it manages to represent a large quantity of attributes and instances in a single screen and allows the user to immediately identify possible patterns, trends, and relationships among the attributes. See an example in Fig. 4.6.

An interesting property of this type of representation is the possibility for the user to interact with the visualization to

- change the order of the columns,
- hide or show columns,
- sort the data by the values of a column,
- show the values of some instances without losing the context of the entire visualization.

An example is shown in Fig. 4.7, where the data are sorted by the values of the first column on the left, by simply clicking on the heading of the column of the values to be sorted, and the data of some instances are made visible by clicking on the rows of the values to be visualized.

4.2.4 Parallel Sets

The geometric techniques discussed so far can be used with any type of attribute (quantitative, ordinal, or categorical). As we have already seen in Section 2.1.2, the

---

[2] It is fitting to recall that the creator of this type of application was Dan Bricklin, who invented VisiCalc, the first spreadsheet application for the Apple II personal computer.

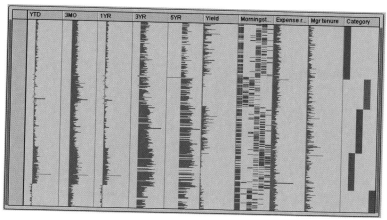

Fig. 4.6 TableLens representation. Image generated by ©Business Objects TableLens software.

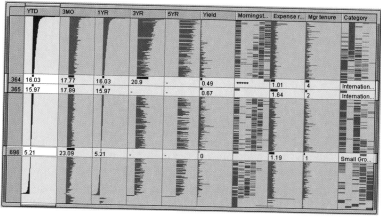

Fig. 4.7 TableLens sorted by the values of the first column on the left. Image generated by ©Business Objects TableLens software.

quantitative type attributes find a natural mapping onto the axes (in the case of parallel coordinates and scatterplots) or into the length of horizontal bars (in the case of TableLens), in that the values are reported on the axis in an order that corresponds to the order of the data; in the case of ordinal or categorical data, it is necessary to find a mapping that divides the available spaces into a discrete collection of subregions. For example, in Fig. 4.3, the production countries of the automobiles are positioned on the last axis to the right of the parallel coordinates, dividing the space uniformly and mapping the production countries on this axis.

Systems specifically created for the representation of categorical data are rarely proposed. Among these, we can mention *parallel sets*, a technique developed by a group of researchers from the VRVis Institute of Vienna [36]. Parallel sets take inspiration from the parallel coordinates but, in contrast, the *frequency* of the values

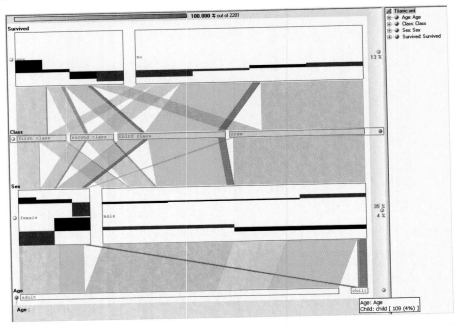

Fig. 4.8 Representation of the datasets of the Titanic disaster using parallel sets. Image reproduced with the permission of Helwig Hauser, VRVis Zentrum für Virtual Reality und Visualisierung Forschungs-GmbH, Vienna.

in the dataset substitutes for the representation of each single instance. This type of representation, unlike the parallel coordinates, turns out to be more appropriate in the case of categorical data and, due to the aggregation of frequency data, it manages to process very large datasets without the problem of space we have seen with parallel coordinates.

Let's see how it works with an example. Fig. 4.8 shows a representation in parallel sets of a dataset derived from the victims of the Titanic disaster, following a collision with an iceberg on the night of April 14, 1912. The dataset has four dependent attributes: the age of the passengers, the sex, the class in which they traveled, and whether they survived the disaster. The layout is reminiscent of the parallel coordinates, but, in this case, the axes have been replaced by a number of rectangular boxes that represent the categories. The width of these rectangles corresponds to the frequency of the corresponding category (for example, in the zone that represents the sex, there were 470 female passengers and 1,731 male passengers; the size of the rectangle reflects this proportion very clearly). Also, quantitative attributes can be mapped onto the axes, as we can see in the case of age. The attributes arranged next to each other are linked by connections that, in this case, represent the values of the frequencies in which the conditions are verified. For example, in the figure, the attribute at the top, survivors, is subdivided into two areas: yes, no. The survivors of the disaster are positioned in relationship to the passenger class to which they belong. For each class item two connections link the areas "yes" and "no" of the survivors, showing the percentage of survivors in each class. The figure very clearly shows that most of the first-class passengers survived, while the majority of the third-class passengers and the crew perished in the disaster. Besides the frequency for every single category, the rectangular block can also contain a histogram that shows, through appropriate statistical calculation, the degree of dependence of each value in the category with the values in the other category with which it is put in relation. The greater the dependence, the larger the histogram.

4.3 Icon Techniques

Another family of techniques of representation of multivariate data that uses the geometric properties of a figure is called *icon techniques*. The name comes from the fact that a geometric figure (an icon, which in this case is also called *glyph*) can have a number of features that may vary: color, shape, size, orientation, etc. The basic idea consists of associating each attribute with a feature in the geometric figure and mapping the data to the extensive properties of each feature. We will examine two well-known techniques: *star plots* and *Chernoff faces*.

4.3.1 Star Plots

A simple and relatively intuitive geometric figure is represented by a star-shaped polygon, whose vertices are defined by a collection of axes that all have the same origin (see Fig. 4.9). Every instance of the dataset can be represented by a "star" in which the values of each attribute of the instance are mapped to the length of each vertex. By joining the points that correspond to each vertex, a geometric figure is obtained, whose shape globally describes the instance of the dataset.

This technique, called a *star plot* (or also a *star glyph*), can be useful for comparing different instances of a dataset, by simply comparing the polygonal shapes derived from each glyph. In Fig. 4.10, we can, for example, compare the statistical data of some climatic values represented by a star plot. The attributes represented are the average annual precipitation, the average annual temperatures, the average maximum annual temperatures, the average minimum annual temperatures, the record for the maximum temperature and the record for the minimum temperature. These data come from the `weatherbase.com` website, which compiles multiyear statistics (reported in tabular version in Table 4.1). The various attributes are mapped to the length of each vertex of the star starting from the right and proceeding counterclockwise.

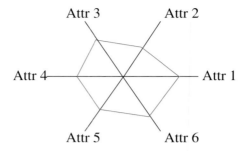

Fig. 4.9 Star plot.

City	Precip. average	Temp. average	Temp. max average	Temp. min average	Record max	Record min
Athens	37	17	21	13	42	−3
Bucharest	58	11	16	5	49	−23
Canberra	62	12	19	6	42	−10
Dublin	74	10	12	6	28	−7
Helsinki	63	5	8	1	31	−36
Hong Kong	218	23	25	21	37	2
London	75	10	13	5	35	−13
Madrid	45	13	20	7	40	−10
Mexico City	63	17	23	11	32	−3
Moscow	59	4	8	1	35	−42
New York	118	12	17	8	40	−18
Porto	126	14	18	10	34	−2
Rio de Janeiro	109	25	30	20	43	7
Rome	80	15	20	11	37	−7
Tunis	44	18	23	13	46	−1
Zurich	107	9	12	6	35	−20

Table 4.1 Annual climatic values in Celsius of some world cities. Values from http://www.weatherbase.com.

From the star plot representation in Fig. 4.10, we notice that Moscow and Helsinki have similar climatic characteristics, as do Athens and Tunis. By simply comparing the shapes generated by the star plot, we are able to visually distinguish grouping of elements of different datasets.

An obvious limit to this type of representation lies in the scalability: For a number of elements that is not exceedingly high, the space occupied on the screen immediately becomes so dense that it is difficult to clearly make out the various iconic forms. Furthermore, the icon techniques are applicable when the qualitative, and not the quantitative, aspect of the various attributes of the dataset is to be explored.

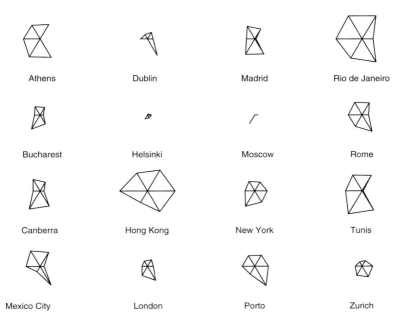

Fig. 4.10 Star plot of the annual climatic data of some cities. Image generated by the S-PLUS tool.

4.3.2 Chernoff Faces

Herman Chernoff put forward an interesting icon technique in which the element of representation is not an inexpressive and dull polygon, but a "face" [10]. Since humans are particularly capable of, and used to, recognizing even the slightest alteration in human facial expressions, Chernoff proposed mapping the attributes of a collection of multivariate data to the form, dimensions, and orientation of human facial features, like the eyes, nose, mouth, ears, etc. Fig. 4.12 gives an example of representation, through Chernoff faces, of the climatic data of the cities we have observed. The mapping is displayed in Fig. 4.11.

Like the star plot, with this representation we are able to deduce similarities between the cities of Helsinki and Moscow and Athens and Tunis. This type of mapping utilizes familiar facial features and is immediately perceptible to us, adding greater expressive power than the star plot. For example, having chosen to map the area of the face to the average precipitation of the city, we immediately see how Hong Kong is a very rainy city. The choice of mapping between attributes and elements of the face is critical and, if badly carried out, can lead to incorrect observations. For example, having chosen to map the width and curvature of the mouth to the record minimum and maximum temperature, respectively, we are incorrectly led

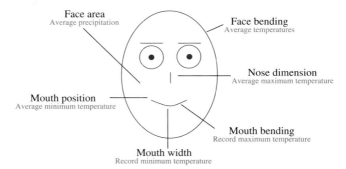

Fig. 4.11 Chernoff face.

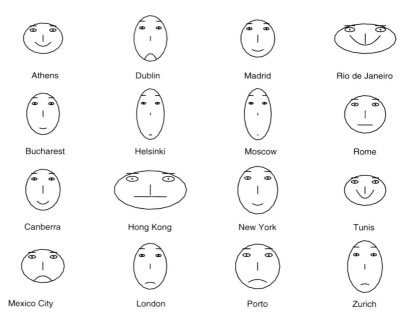

Fig. 4.12 Climatic data of some cities represented by Chernoff faces. Image generated by the S-PLUS statistics tool.

to understand that cities like Rio de Janeiro and Tunis have better climatic conditions than the others, just because the face has a smiling expression.

This type of representation is very interesting because of its way of presenting data, even though it has been criticized over the years by numerous visualization experts, in that the symmetry of parts like the eyes, eyebrows, and ears, present in pairs on the face, build an unnecessary duplication that is not actually present, for instance, in the star plot. Furthermore, studies have shown how the choice of mapping of an attribute can bring about differences of up to 25% in terms of cluster perception in the dataset. This means that to classify two faces as "similar" is widely influenced by the choice of mapping a specific attribute to one facial feature instead of another.

4.4 Pixel-Oriented Techniques

To maximize the number of elements to represent, some techniques use the pixels of the screen as basic units of representation. In effect, the pixel represents the smallest part, the "atomic" unit, beyond which it is impossible to subdivide the representation. A computer screen with a $1,024 \times 768$ pixels resolution could therefore potentially represent $786,432$ separate elements of a univariate dataset, mapping the data of an attribute to the color of the pixel of the corresponding element. This way we obtain a upper limit of visible elements in a single screen, beyond which it is theoretically impossible to go. In practice, this limit is never reached, first because part of the screen is dedicated to containing functional and aesthetic elements of the representation such as buttons, borders, text elements, and others; second, because there is a very limited number of situations in which it is sufficient to map a unit of information to the color of a single pixel of the screen.

Let's look at how to apply these techniques to a collection of multivariate data. The goal consists of representing the greatest amount of data in a single screen, mapping each value into the color of a pixel of the screen and grouping the data that belong to a certain attribute in a specific area, called a *window*. Daniel Keim [31] has studied the approach from a theoretical point of view and has defined a series of factors that need to be considered when applying this technique:

- *Shape of the window.* Usually represented in rectangular shapes and arranged in a matrix on the screen. Other shapes have been proposed, but the rectangle remains the most suitable to best take advantage of the screen's physical space.
- *Visual mapping.* What does each pixel represent?
- *Arrangement of the pixels.* How should the pixels be arranged in each window?
- *Color mapping.* How should the colors of the pixels be mapped?
- *Ordering of the windows.* In what order are the windows arranged in the screen's physical space?

As an example of such applications, Fig. 4.13 shows a tool for monitoring the use of online courses in an e-learning platform [41]. The e-learning platforms are, by now, a very common tool in universities. For management or statistical purposes, it can be extremely useful to comprehend the level of the students' use of each online course. The problem is that a platform can run hundreds (or even thousands) of courses, and, therefore, tracking the level of use of each course can be very taxing and complicated. The application shown in Fig. 4.13 serves precisely this purpose. This is a sort of dashboard of the use of resources in the e-learning platform. The main window is subdivided into a control area (right) and a matrix of little windows

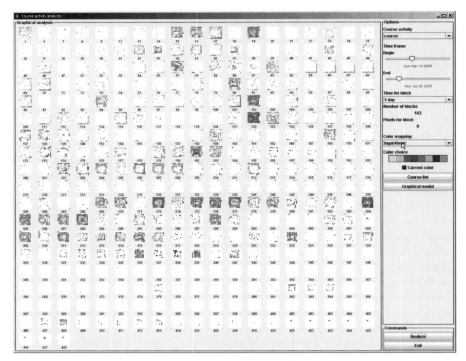

Fig. 4.13 Example of an application that uses the pixel as a basic unit. Image published in [41] and reproduced with the permission of Springer.

(left). Each window represents an online course run by the platform, while the pixels represent a unit of time (1 minute, 1 hour, 1 day, etc.). The pixels are distributed according to a *temporal spiral*, with the first pixel (based on order of time) arranged in the center of the little windows, then extending to the edges in a clockwise direction.

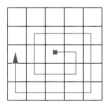

The pixels are colored according to the amount of use of the course during the time corresponding to the pixel. A color scale is used with a single hue (blue), and intensity represents the use of the course in that unit of time: A light color means little course use (completely white corresponds to no activity) and a strong blue color, on the other hand, points to intense use. From Fig. 4.13, which represents as many as 345 courses in a single screen, it is clear which courses have had the most activity during the semester. By analyzing the positioning of the colored pixels in detail, it

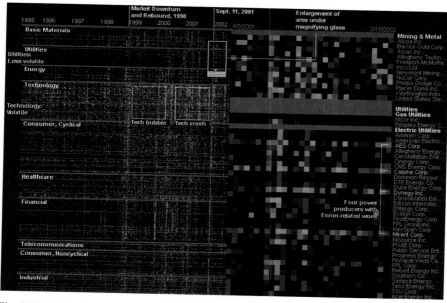

Fig. 4.14 Market Radar is an application managed by SmartMoney for analyzing the stock market share history. Image reproduced with the permission of ©smartmoney.com.

is possible to understand if the activities were concentrated at the start or the end of the semester, or if they are distributed throughout the semester. The advantages of this approach are notable, not only for the quantity of data that we manage to represent in a single screen, but also for the simplicity of the interpretation, which, from a cognitive point of view, does not call for particular effort.

Another interesting example is *Market Radar*, produced by SmartMoney,[3] a company that offers stock market share investors a wide number of analytical tools that use modern techniques for the visual representation of information. Market Radar analyzes the history of shares quoted on the U.S. stock exchange (Fig. 4.14). It visualizes the price variation of 500 shares over the last 8 years, making it possible to examine the entire market dynamic, over a substantially long period of time, at a glance. Market Radar takes the weekly price variations into account: Each week is represented by a column in the left part of the figure, while a different row of the matrix corresponds to each stock price.

Stocks are grouped in sectors, to study the progress of the various types of sectors or industries. Each weekly price change is represented by a dot in the matrix on the left: green if the stock went up in that week, red if it went down, while the intensity of the color reflects the variation with respect to the previous week. In the example reported in this figure, it is clearly noticeable how the shares belonging to the technology sector have the highest instability, characterized by abrupt highs

---

[3] http://www.smartmoney.com.

and lows in very short periods of time. It is also easy to make out the periods of strong growth in this sector around 1999 (with a prevalence of green pixels), and a successive period of serious crisis for all technology departments after the first half of 2000.

The user can put a sort of magnifying glass on a particular area in the matrix, enabling the observation of the magnified detail on the right, where the performance of every company can be clearly distinguished. The example shown in the figure displays an extremely negative week for most stocks, corresponding to the attack on the Twin Towers in New York on September 11, 2001.

4.5 Conclusion

In this chapter, we have described some of the most common techniques used to represent multivariate data, which characterize the vast majority of real-world problems. The challenge is to visually represent multidimensional data in a two-dimensional screen space. This limitation obliges us to resort to a trick in order to map several attributes into spatial substrates and graphical elements. We divided these techniques into three categories: geometric, iconic, and pixel-based (depending on the main approach adopted), showing some applications that have reached a good level of adoption in the market.

Chapter 5
Networks and Hierarchies

All datasets considered in the previous chapters are organized in the form of simple tables that, following the process of visualization described in Section 2.1, have been converted into a visual representation. This visual representation, if well designed, with a proper elicitation of users' needs, can be adopted by a particular type of user to carry out specific tasks.

However, not all datasets we deal with in the real world have a linear structure: Just think of the city transport network, or the organization of the staff in a company. These cases involve data that, by their nature, have a very particular and important characteristic, that of *relation* (or *connection*) and/or of *enclosure* (or *containment*). In an urban transport network, the main elements, the bus stops or subway stations, are **connected** by means of the bus or subway lines. Within a company, each employee **belongs** to a specific unit or sector, under the direction of another company employee. Data structured through relationships (such as the urban transport network) are said to be organized in a *network* system, as the relationships between the elements can be thought as a network made up of connected elements. Data in which each element of the system (except for the top element) is a subordinate to a single other element are said to be organized *hierarchically*, by the hierarchy that is derived from placing the element that contains all the other elements at the top and descending step by step, with the contained elements immediately below the containing one.

The structural properties of these data types are crucial to understanding how the dataset is organized and are often the foremost aspects that must be made clear through visual representations. The properties of relation and enclosure can be represented very simply and intuitively by graphs and trees, illustrated in the following sections.

R. Mazza, *Introduction to Information Visualization*,
DOI: 10.1007/978-1-84800-219-7_5, © Springer-Verlag London Limited 2009

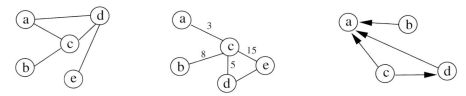

Fig. 5.1 Examples of graphs. On the left is a normal graph, in the center is a graph in which each edge is given a numerical value, and to the right is a directed graph.

5.1 Network Data

The data organized in a network structure can be naturally represented by *graphs*. Graphs are those visual representations in which the points, called *nodes* or *vertices*, represent instances of the data. Nodes are correlated by connections, called *edges*, which represent relationships between the instances. The edges of the graphs can also have direction (in this case, we speak of *directed graphs*) and values, which are called *weights* (in the case of numerical values) or *labels* (in the case of textual descriptions). Examples of graphs are represented in Fig. 5.1.

For a long time, graphs have been studied in mathematics and information technology (think, for example, of the *graph theory* or of the *finite-state automata*) and are naturally suited to representing entities where there is a network organization to represent. The following are issues to consider when representing structured data through a graph [8]:

1. *Positioning of nodes.* Information visualization graphs often represent abstract data types that don't have a natural spatial location. It is necessary to decide on which criteria to arrange the nodes in the space (that is, the *layout*). Some techniques, such as *multidimensional scaling* (MDS) [18], can convert a collection of multivariate data (of any dimension), mapping them into one, two, or three dimensions, from which the Cartesian coordinates are derived to position the nodes in the space. Some layout techniques will be illustrated later. Moreover, we can decide to map some attributes to the shape, color, and dimension of the nodes.
2. *Representation of the edges.* A relationship between two nodes has to be represented by an edge. These can have associated weights and can be direct or indirect. The weights can be indicated next to the edges or mapped to the color or to the width of the edge.
3. *Dimensioning.* Some datasets can have thousands or even millions of records, which can't be directly represented by graphs in a one-to-one relationship with nodes and edges. It is necessary to find solutions in such cases.
4. *Interaction with graphs.* Modern visual representation software allows the user to interact with the generated view, which is very helpful when we deal with complex graphs with a high number of nodes and edges. The user can manipulate the representation of a graph to move the nodes, zoom in on a part of the graph, and hide or show edges or even a part of the graph.

We will show some examples illustrating the use of graphs to represent data organized in a network structure in various contexts, and we'll see how these factors have been handled within the various applications.

5.1.1 Concept Maps and Mind Maps

Concept maps , proposed by Joseph Novak at the beginning of the 1970s, are diagrammatic representations showing the relationships among concepts of a complex and structured domain. They are built from a series of concepts (*semantic nodes*), which then proceed to their connections by means of labeled edges (*propositions*) that describe the type of connection. It is also possible to begin from a general concept, associating it, little by little, to more specific concepts, to have a sufficiently detailed description of the domain. It is possible to create maps for any type of subject: a website, a book, a service, a product, etc. The concept maps are best used in teaching, as they manage to outline the structured knowledge in a very synthetic and reasoned manner. Fig. 5.2 depicts a concept map describing the "website" concept.
1

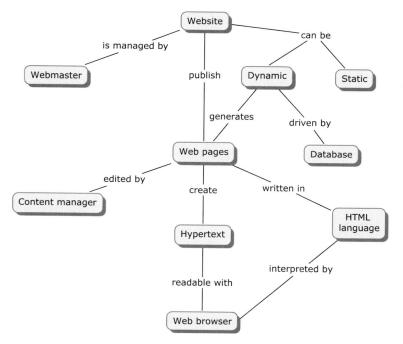

Fig. 5.2 Example of a concept map that describes concepts regarding a website.

---

1 The map was created using the IHMC Cmap software tool; http://cmap.ihmc.us.

Mind maps are similar to concept maps. These are used to describe ideas, situations, projects, organizations, etc. by graphical associations. These find many applications in brainstorming sessions, in educational environments, or when organizing ideas. For example, when attending a lesson or presentation, an effective mnemonic and organizational technique consists of tracing the most important concepts in a graphical-textual manner and associating them to each other, graphically, through logic-associative relationships. Mind maps are usually organized by starting from a central concept, from which more correlated nodes are emitted, which will then be further specialized and divided. What distinguishes the mind map from the concept map is, therefore, the fact of having a single topic as a starting point (as opposed to concept maps, which can have many), besides having a radial structure, where the nodes develop from a base subject, according to a number of levels, whereas concept maps are based on connections between concepts. An example of a mind map, which represents the early ideas for the preparation of a university course, is illustrated in Fig. 5.3.[2] Recently, Tony Buzan, the English researcher who coined the term "mind map," tried to theorize this approach, designing a number of rules and best practice to use the mind map, such as the use of colors, images, symbols, and various character sizes. For a complete treatment, consult [7].

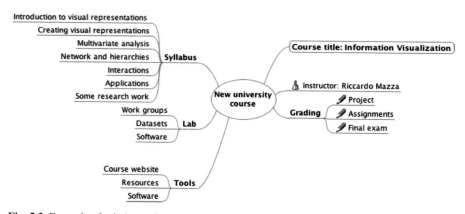

Fig. 5.3 Example of mind map for the planning of a university course.

5.1.2 Complex Network Data

Graphs are a very efficient form of representation for network data, but unfortunately they have the disadvantage of not being very scalable: By increasing the number of nodes, the graph becomes too complex and not very readable. The graph in Fig. 5.4 describes the network of social relationships among a number of individuals. Each

---

[2] The map was realized using FreeMind software; http://freemind.sourceforge.net.

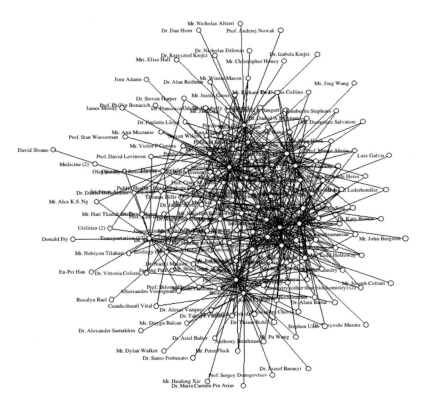

Fig. 5.4 An example of a complex graph.

node represents an individual, while the edges represent social relationships among these individuals, such as family, friends, colleagues, or acquaintances. Visual representations of this type, called *social networks*, are important to understand social relationships among various individuals, and to determine qualitative aspects such as leadership or informal structure. The problem of the representation in this figure is the density of nodes and edges concentrated in a small space, which makes it impossible to distinguish among the graphical elements placed in the center of the figure.

There is a great deal of ongoing research into the problem of complex graphs. Periodically, new methodologies are proposed to increase the number of nodes representable in a graph, or to improving their legibility. These problems can be tackled by adopting one or more of the following strategies:

- using new geometric arrangements (layout) for the graph design in order to improve the readability,

- approximating the structure with a reduced, but more readable, graph; for instance, by reducing the number of edges displayed on the graph or by hiding relationships of lesser interest after they are displayed,
- adding interactivity to the software that generates the visual representations to generate dynamic graphs, which can be manipulated and explored according to the user's needs.

Interactive techniques will be the subject of the following chapter. Here we will illustrate some examples of how geometric arrangements and approximations, which are required to produce more readable graphs, have been applied.

5.1.2.1 Optimizing Layout

The basic problem in representing a graph with a very large number of nodes is that these often have such a large number of crossing edges that it becomes impossible for the user to perceive the graph's general structure. The ideal would be to arrange the nodes in the space so as to minimize the number of crossing edges. The most common layout techniques that attempt to optimize the positioning of the nodes are called *spring-embedder* [17] and *force-directed* [22]. These techniques use algorithms that position the nodes of a graph in two- or three-dimensional space so that all the edges are of more or less equal length and there are as few crossing edges as possible. The resulting graph also has good aesthetic properties (uniform edge length, uniform edge distribution, and some symmetry). Figure 5.5 represents a graph, created by Jeffrey Heer's tool, *prefuse*,[3] that shows a social network making use of a *force-directed* algorithm.

5.1.2.2 Reducing Graph Complexity

When the number of nodes is very large (such as a data structure with tens of thousands of nodes), geometric techniques also show their limits, both for the reduced space of the screen and for the complexity of the layout algorithms, that would require longer computation time. The only possibility we have of visualizing a graph that could be of some use to the user is to create a "reduced" version of the graph, meaning approximating it with a scaled-down version that sacrifices the information somewhat, but simultaneously ends up being more readable and keeps the global structure of the data, allowing identification of the main patterns. To allow for a good final visual representation of the graph, it is necessary to attempt to reduce the number of objects represented and, at the same time, preserve the global structure of the graph (that is usually the main point of interest for analysis). A very simple technique, called *link reduction*, consists of visualizing only the edges having weights above a certain value, or that satisfy specific criteria. In this way, only the edges that could be of interest to the user are represented.

---

[3] http://www.prefuse.org/.

Fig. 5.5 An example of a graph that uses a force-directed algorithm to represent a social network. Image created with the prefuse tool and reproduced with the permission of Jeffrey Heer, University of California, Berkeley.

Other, more sophisticated techniques, such as the *minimum spanning trees (MST)* and *pathfinder network scaling (PFNET)* techniques, analyze the topological structure of the nodes and edges to eliminate the redundant edges and maintain the most significant links. Represented in Fig. 5.6 are a complete graph (left) and its reduced version (right), using the *pathfinder* technique.

To reduce the complexity of a graph, one can also intervene by attempting to diminish the number of nodes visualized. There are *clustering* techniques that can be applied to data to be represented by graphs. These techniques tend to visualize a group of "similar" nodes by combining them in one node (the *cluster*) to reduce the number of nodes and edges to be visualized. The degree of "similarity" between two nodes depends on the application type and the domain of the data visualized through the graph.

Some solutions have been studied specifically for generating and managing graphs with an extremely high number of nodes. These solutions use a combination of layout techniques, approximation, and interaction. One of these, NicheWorks [67], is able to treat up to a million nodes in a few minutes. It deals with a prototype developed at Bell Lab (now *Alcatel-Lucent*) in the mid-1990s, with the aim of exploring a visual approach to the study of telephone frauds. The algorithm was then generalized for generic problems, where there is a need to visualize graphs with a

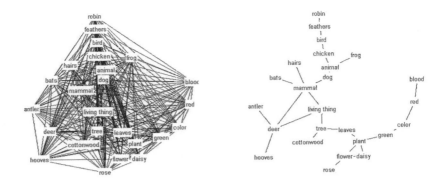

Fig. 5.6 Complete graph (left) and the reduced link version (right), achieved using the pathfinder technique. Graphs were generated with the KNOT analysis tool. Images courtesy of Interlink.

large number of nodes, and applied to other domains. NicheWorks uses radial positioning to optimize the positioning of the nodes in the space, in a way that avoids the crossing edges and sets a high number of nodes in the visible space. Furthermore, the weights associated with the edges are taken into consideration in the construction of the graph, so that the nodes are positioned at a distance inversely proportional to the weights of the edges that connect them (meaning the higher the values of the weights that connect two nodes, the closer the nodes are).

Figure 5.7 shows three types of layouts proposed by NicheWorks:

- *Circular layout.* The nodes are arranged circularly in the immediate periphery of a single circle.
- *Hexagonal grid.* The nodes are arranged at the grid points of a regular hexagonal grid.

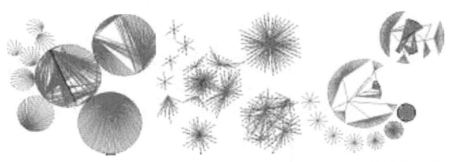

Fig. 5.7 Main NicheWorks layouts: circular (left), hexagonal (center), and tree (right). Image by [67]; Reprinted with permission from *The Journal of Computational and Graphical Statistics.* ©1999 by the American Statistical Association. All rights reserved.

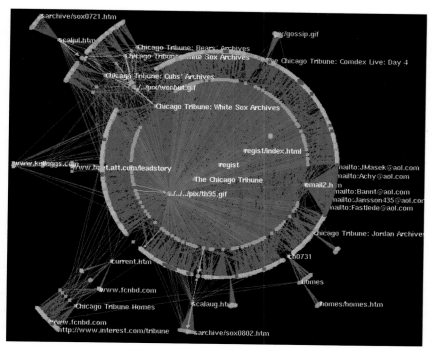

Fig. 5.8 NicheWorks shows the graph of the *Chicago Tribune's* website structure. Image reproduced with the permission of Graham Wills, SPSS Inc.

- *Tree layout.* The nodes are arranged with the root node at the center, around which each node is arranged on a circle. This type of layout is appropriate for hierarchical structures but can also be applied to network data.

NicheWorks has been used to study fraudulent international telephone calls [14] and to analyze complex website structures. Fig. 5.8 displays a graph of the structure of the pages and internal links, back in 1997, of the Chicago Tribune's website, one of Chicago's major daily newspapers. The goal of the representation is to understand how the website was structured and to see which design criteria were used in its production. The graph was represented using the tree layout (see Fig. 5.7). The shape and the color of the nodes have the following mapping:

- orange square: local pages,
- orange circle: local images,
- blue square: external pages,
- yellow square: program interface for managing forms or dynamic pages (CGI).

Some of the most important nodes are labelled. The graph shows the entrance pages of the site (positioned at the center of the figure) that link to a local page (internal circle). These pages contain a connection to further dynamic pages (external circle). Therefore, a structure of three levels (main page of the website, internal circle, and external circle) globally dominate. Only a limited number of pages have a different structure (top left of the image), which are mainly the pages dealing with sports subjects.

The advantage of approaches based on visual representations, as opposed to the automatic analysis techniques such as those that use *data mining* algorithms,[4] lies in their flexibility and the human visual system's ability to adapt. According to the authors of NicheWorks [14], people who attempt to defraud telephone companies adopt systems that elude the systematic checks that are carried out on international calls. The use of visualization systems can instead be adapted dynamically to allow recognition of possible changes that are then used by the perpetrators of these abuses.

5.1.3 Geographic Representations

Often graphs are used to describe the topology of networks in which a spatial or geographic component is present. In this case, this component is used to position the nodes in the space. For example, we are used to representing telecommunication networks with graphs, where we match a physical component to the nodes: a server, router, hub, etc., while the edges represent the connections (physical or virtual) among the various elements of the network. Frequently, the nodes have a wide-scale geographic positioning, which must be depicted visually. Figure 5.9 uses a layer technique to represent the geographic coverage that the backbone NSFNET T1 served during September 1991 [12]. The backbone and the connections with the various cities are visually differentiated by the raised layer of the geographic map, so as to create a clear visual separation between the network and the territory. A color scale that goes from purple (zero bytes) to white (100 million bytes) indicates the volume of incoming traffic measured at every point served by the backbone.

Other examples of a network topology on a world scale are represented in Fig. 5.10 by SeeNet [13], a result of the work directed by Stephen Eick at Bell Labs. SeeNet visualized the amount of Internet traffic throughout 50 nations, measured by the NSFNET backbone in 1993.

However, these types of representations are often appreciated more for their "aesthetic" value than for their effective use, so much so that they have been collected and published on a website, *The Atlas of Cyberspaces*, as well as appearing in a successful publication written by Martin Dodge and Rob Kitchin [32].

---

[4] The *data mining* algorithms seek to extract useful information from large quantities of data automatically or semiautomatically. They look for patterns in the data to hypothesize on causal type relationships between phenomena tied to the data.

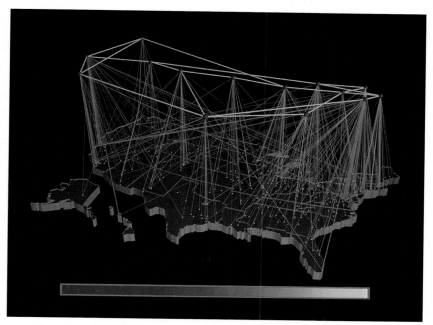

Fig. 5.9 An image that shows the topology of the NSFNET T1 backbone network in September 1991 in the United States. The situation today is certainly more complex than that represented in the figure. Created by D. Cox and R. Patterson/NCSA, UIUC. © 1994 The Board of Trustees of the University of Illinois.

5.1.4 Transport Networks

A very common example of information represented in graphical form is the transport networks, represented on a geographic map, in which the cities connected by the railway lines are highlighted. There is, however, a very particular type of transport representation: the maps of the underground train. Figure 5.11 shows a representation of a (unofficial) map of the Madrid Metro network. This type of map was conceived of in 1931 by Harry Beck, a London public transport employee, who, in his free time, designed the first draft of what is used today as the model of public transport networks all over the world. He proposed a new type of map inspired by the electrical circuit systems. His genial intuition was to understand that a traveler wants to know how to reach a destination when leaving from a specific station, and is not interested in the physical position of the stations. What matters is the topology of the network, or how the various stations are connected and which lines to take to reach a certain destination. In this way, Madrid Metro map represented in Fig. 5.11, is not a "map" in the true sense of the term, since the proportions of the physical distances between the stations are not respected. Rather, it deals with a graph (or a diagram) in which the lines, stations, and zones of the transport network are represented, and the correspondence with the physical position of the stations has been

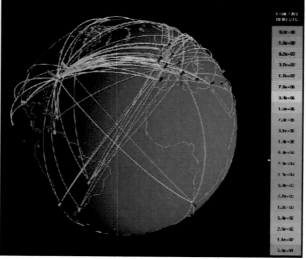

Fig. 5.10 SeeNet, 3D representation of the Internet traffic across the NSFNET backbone network in 1993. Images reproduced with the permission of Stephen Eick, SSS Research, Inc.

distorted, to concentrate the graph in the smallest space possible. It can therefore be called a topological, rather than geographical, map.

5.1.5 3D Graphs

Some modern tools for the construction of graphs are able to generate three-dimensional layouts. In Fig. 5.12, we report two examples generated by Tulip,[5] one of the best toolkits for generating graphs. The 3D layout graph can be turned and

---

[5] http://www.tulip-software.org.

Fig. 5.11 A map of the Madrid Metro system. Images licensed under Creative Commons Share-Alike.

moved, to allow the user to change the view and make visible any objects that could possibly be occluded.

5.2 Hierarchical Data

We speak of hierarchy when considering data characterized by containment properties. Examples of hierarchy are the organization of files and directories in the computer (the files are contained within the directories, which are in turn contained within other directories), the structure of books (organized in parts, chapters, sec-

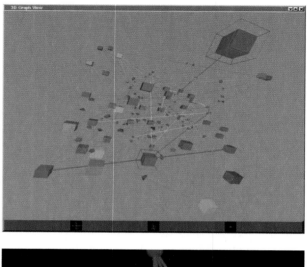

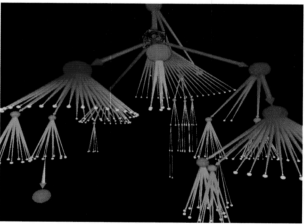

Fig. 5.12 Examples of graphs with three-dimensional layouts generated by Tulip software.

tions, etc.), company organization (president, director, advisors, supervisors, etc.), and the taxonomies used in biology. A hierarchy can be represented through a graph with a starting node called *root*. Each node has zero or more *child nodes*, which are usually represented below the ancestor, and the ancestor is called the *parent node*. A node has one parent, at most. Graphs of this type are defined as *trees*, precisely due to their similarity to actual trees, but in difference to the botanical trees, they are represented upside down, with the root at the top and the leaves at the bottom. An example of a tree is reproduced in figure 5.13, which represents a simplified version of the classification of the wind instruments as proposed in 1914 by Curt Sachs and Erich von Hornbostel.

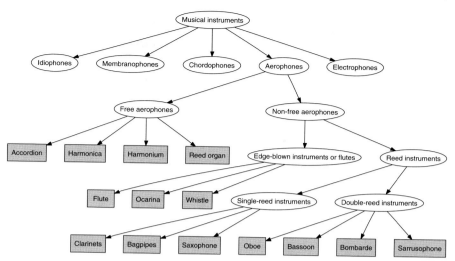

Fig. 5.13 A tree representing the classification of the wind instruments according to Curt Sachs and Erich von Hornbostel.

5.2.1 File System

For anyone who spends a great part of the day working with computers (such as the author of this text), the most familiar hierarchical structure is probably the *file system*, which is the mechanism with which the files are stored and organized on a mass storage device like a hard disk. In the file system, the files are organized hierarchically, starting from a *directory* (or *folder*) called root that contains files or other directories. The file system can be represented both textually (through the shell of the operating system) and graphically, through a file browser. In the visual representation used by all modern operating systems (e.g. Fig. 5.14 of the Apple Mac OS X systems), the folder metaphor, which contains documents (the files) and other folders, is generally used. However, this is a partial representation of the file system, as it may contain tens of thousands of files and directories. Particularly those who have to manage servers with large quantities of data shared among many people, the management of the file system is crucial. The system administrator must have tools that permit efficient monitoring of the file collections on the disk, to be able to identify situations in which system administrator intervention could be required.

As early as the beginning of the 1990s, the first graphical tools were proposed to integrate the command-line interface typical of UNIX-like systems with much more explicative and immediate visualizations. In 1991, Phil Dykstra developed *Xdu*, a system for graphical monitoring of the UNIX file system. Xdu visualizes the results of the UNIX command *du* (which returns some statistics on disk usage)

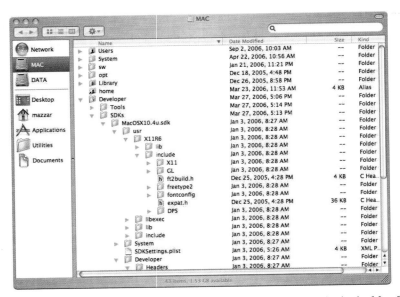

Fig. 5.14 Representation of the file system by the graphical interface Finder in the Mac OS X system.

in graphical form. Fig. 5.15 gives an example created by the *xdiskusage* tool,[6] a modern and improved version of Xdu. A representation with rectangles is used, which are placed into the screen from left to right. The positioning of the rectangles reflects the hierarchy of the file system. Each rectangle corresponds to a directory, and the dimension of the rectangle is mapped to the physical space (bytes) occupied by every directory on the disk.

Other tools have also attempted visualization in 3D dynamics. That was made possible by the availability of increasingly fast 3D graphical boards on personal computers and the availability of powerful graphical languages, like OpenGL. *Fsv*[7] is one of the tools that has been very successful in 3D graphics for navigating a file system. Fsv offers two types of three-dimensional representation: *MapV view*, which returns to the style of xdiskusage but with three-dimensional blocks, and *TreeV view* (see Fig. 5.16), which, instead represents the directory like a "platform," which supports three-dimensional blocks that represent the files contained in it. The captivating fsv visual representation should not deceive us: The system administrators and professionals who manage file systems with great volumes of data have always expressed perplexities about the effective usefulness of these types of visual representations.

---

[6] http://xdiskusage.sourceforge.net/.

[7] http://fsv.sourceforge.net/.

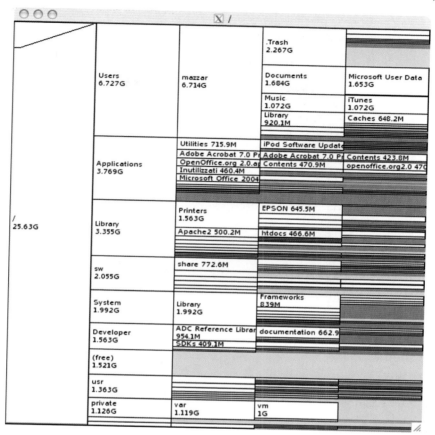

Fig. 5.15 Xdiskusage uses a representation with rectangles of the file system.

5.2.2 Representing Evolutionary Data with Trees

Philology is a science that studies texts, that may have been modified over time, to restore them to their original form. *Textual criticism* of a text consists of attempting to determine its original form through the study of its variations in the course of the process of traditional handwriting and/or print. In philology, trees are often used to represent the variations of a text over time. In fact, before the invention of mechanical printing, the texts were copied by hand (in ancient Egypt, for example, the scribes were specialized in the transcription of holy texts) and often, either by error due to an oversight or for explicit censors, modifications were introduced to the various transcriptions. The copied (and modified) texts could have been used as models to create other copies that may in turn have been subjected to other modifications, and so on. Philology, which attempts to rebuild the original form of a text, analyzes its various versions and pays close attention to the variations. These are based on

Fig. 5.16 Fsv in the TreeV version visualizes the organization of the file system by a metaphor of an interconnected platform (the directory) on which the blocks (the files) are laid. Image reproduced with the permission of Daniel Richard.

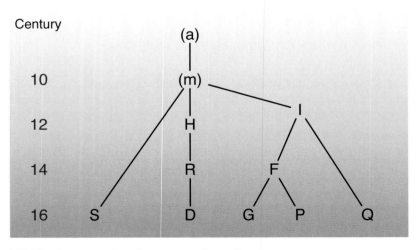

Fig. 5.17 Visual representation of a *stemma codicum* of a text.

the assumption that each copier tended to report the errors of the text that was being used as the model and then introduced some of his own. Another basic principle is that if two different versions of the text share a certain number of unusual errors, then it is very likely that they have a common model. Through this analysis, a tree is created, called *stemma codicum* in philology, that reports the "tradition of the text." An example of stemma codicum treated by a concrete linguistic study, in which an essay on Hippocrates [47] was analyzed, is represented in Fig. 5.17, where the various "witnesses" (manuscripts) that it reports are indicated, taken from the first, original version of the text (a) called *archetype*.

5.2.3 Cone Tree

Cone tree [50] is a three-dimensional visualization technique for hierarchical data developed by Robertson, Mackinlay, and Card at the Xerox PARC laboratories in long ago 1991 (see fig. 5.18). It was developed to represent hierarchies with a large number of nodes. For this reason, a 3D representation, which extends the physical limits of the two-dimensional display, was chosen. The tree is built from the root node, with all the children nodes arranged at equal distances from the parent, to form a semitransparent cone. The process is then repeated for every node of the hierarchy, with the diameter of the base of each cone being reduced at every level, to ensure the arrangement of all nodes in the space. A particular innovation introduced by this application (which is reported here more for historical reasons than for its practicality) is the possibility of being able to rotate the cone to bring the nodes that may be occluded to the foreground, and the possibility of hiding a cone and all that is below. The particular arrangement of the nodes in the cone is worth mentioning, as it allows for the perception of the density of the nodes in each cone, thanks to the use of transparency and the shadow projected on the low level.

5.2.4 Botanical Tree

In 2001, researchers at the Eindhoven University of Technology in Netherlands made an interesting observation. The structure of trees is commonly used to represent data organized hierarchically, but this metaphor does present some limitations when we try to represent organizations of a certain complexity. However, when we observe a real botanical tree, we notice that, even if it has a large number of leaves and branches, we can always make out its various leaves, branches, and general structure. Then why not represent the hierarchical organization similarly to how trees were formed in nature?

Fig 5.19 gives an example of a botanical tree that represents the structure of a file system [33]. It uses a 3D representation to create trees that are reminiscent of botanical trees (in fact, a difference from the trees seen up to now is that the root

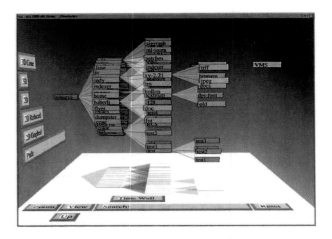

Fig. 5.18 Representation of hierarchical structure by a cone tree. Images reproduced with the permission of Stuart Card, George Robertson and Xerox PARC.

node is placed at the bottom, as opposed to at the top), and for this reason the fruits are visualized, as opposed to the simple leaves. In the example in Fig. 5.19, each fruit represents a collection of files, to avoid cluttering effects that can be generated by a high number of leaves. Each fruit has some colored "spots," which correspond to a file; the area and the color of these spots are mapped to the dimension and file type, respectively.

Fig. 5.19 Botanical tree. Image courtesy of Jack van Wijk, Eindhoven University of Technology.

5.2.5 Treemap

In 1990, Ben Shneiderman, one of the most active researchers in the human–computer interaction and information visualization, found himself facing the problem of a full hard disk on one of his servers at the University of Maryland. Shneiderman had to find a way to determine which were the biggest files that could be canceled and who of the 14 users of the server made the most use of the space on the disk. He was unsatisfied with the analysis tools available at the time (everything was more or less based on tree-type representations), he studied an alternative to be able to visualize the hierarchy of the files on the disk. It was then that he had the brilliant idea of using a space-filling technique called *treemap* [51]. Even today, the treemap is one of the most widely used visualization techniques for hierarchical data, used in dozens of applications.

The technique is called *space filling* because it uses all the available space, displaying hierarchical data using nested rectangles. The screen space is divided into rectangles starting from the root node, and then each rectangle is further divided for

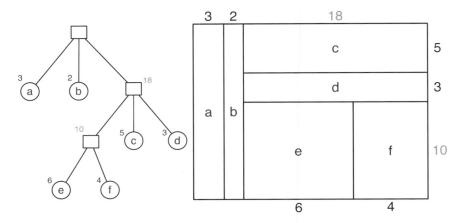

Fig. 5.20 On the left is an example of a tree representation, where a numerical value is associated with each leaf. The internal nodes report the sum of the values of the nodes below. On the right is the treemap representation of the tree.

each level of the hierarchy, until all components of the hierarchy are placed. We'll show how this technique works, in its original 1992 conception version, by applying it to an example.

A tree structure is represented on the left of figure 5.20. In this structure, the values are associated with the leaf nodes (we can think of it as a structure of directories, where a file corresponds to each leaf having a value that corresponds to the dimension of the file). The algorithm of construction of the treemap proceeds recursively, starting from the root node and considering the nodes derived from it. The example that we are observing has a root node from which three nodes derive: node *a* with a value of 3, node *b* with a value of 2, and an internal node with a total value (that is the sum of all the values below) of 18. The algorithm therefore partitions the available space into three rectangles (see Fig. 5.20, right): a rectangle for *a*, a rectangle for *b*, and another rectangle for the internal node assigned to the containment of the nodes below. The blocks are created by partitioning the area vertically in such a way that the proportions of the values are respected. Then the successive nodes continue, although the space is partitioned horizontally this time. The blocks are created in this way for nodes *c*, *d* and the additional internal node. The algorithm carries on analyzing all the levels of the tree, always partitioning the remaining space in an area proportional to the value, alternating horizontal and vertical positioning for every level of the tree.

Fig. 5.21 represents an example generated by version 4.1 of treemap software, developed at the University of Maryland.[8] The figure represents a visualization that shows the cases of mortality in 43 types of pathologies, organized according to the hierarchy defined by the *International Community Health Services* (ICHS), with data taken in the United States in 1998. The size of the rectangles indicates the per-

---

[8] The software can be downloaded from http://www.cs.umd.edu/hcil/treemap

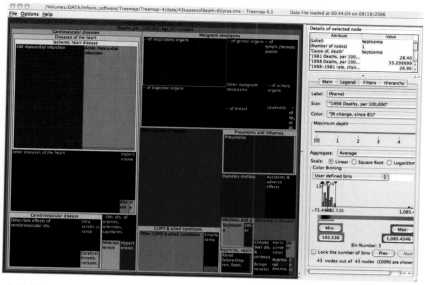

Fig. 5.21 Treemap that represents cases of mortality in 43 types of pathologies. Image reproduced with the permission of Ben Shneiderman, University of Maryland, Human–Computer Interaction Lab.

centage of deaths per 100,000 inhabitants, while the color indicates the percentage of variation found from 1981 to 1998. As can be deduced from the figure, cardio-vascular diseases are the main cause of death, but the green coloration indicates that the cases are decreasing (in particular, there was a 41% decrease from 1981 to 1998), while it is the contrary for other rarer diseases, such as Alzheimer's, for ex-ample, which, with its purple coloring, presents the maximum increase (which was 1,085%).

This technique is very efficient for representing hierarchical data, where the rep-resentation of the nodes through the dimension and color of blocks helps the user to immediately single out and compare nodes, individualize patterns, and identify exceptions.

Over the years, algorithms that generate this type of representation are constantly being improved, with a certain number of layouts available [4], and have produced innumerable applications that use this captivating technique to represent data of all types. We'll show two applications that have attained a good level of success: NewsMap, Map of the Market, and Sequoia View.

5.2.5.1 Newsmap

In 2004, Marcos Weskamp developed an innovative modality of presenting the news from Google News. The application is called Newsmap and is visible in real time by

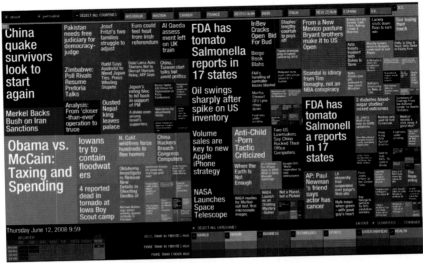

Fig. 5.22 Newsmap uses a treemap algorithm to represent news from Google News U.S. on June 12, 2008. Image reproduced with the permission of Marcos Weskamp.

connecting to the website http://marumushi.com/apps/newsmap. Figure 5.22 shows the interface screen that visualizes the news coverage for Google News on June 12, 2008. The color defines the type of news (e.g., sport, entertainment, reports) and the size indicates how many articles deal with each story, from all of the sources considered by Google News. This application, thus, assigns some criteria of importance to the number of sources that report the news, assuming that the more important the news, the more it is present in the various journalistic sources. The intensity of color is also taken advantage of to understand how recent the information is: Recent news has a light coloring, while less recent news has a darker coloring.

5.2.5.2 Map of the Market

SmartMoney's Map of the Market (http://www.smartmoney.com/map-of-the-market) application was inspired by treemaps, to visualize the variations in stock exchange shares of over 500 stock markets in a single screen (Fig. 5.23). Map of the Market has attained notable success thanks to its very compact and elegant representation of a remarkable number of share titles, which provides a collective vision of progress for the entire shares market through a single map and, at the same time, allows visualization of the details of every share title. By using a colored rectangle visualization, organized hierarchically according to the 11 sectors (health care, finance, energy, technology, etc.), and grouped according to the industry type (e.g., the technological sector is further subdivided into software, hardware, Internet, telecommunications, semiconductors, and peripherals), the map automatically updates every 15

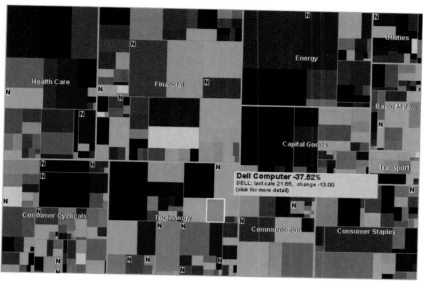

Fig. 5.23 Smartmoney.com Map of the Market. The map reports the variations during the past year on the national market on June 14, 2006. Image reproduced with the permission of ©SmartMoney.com.

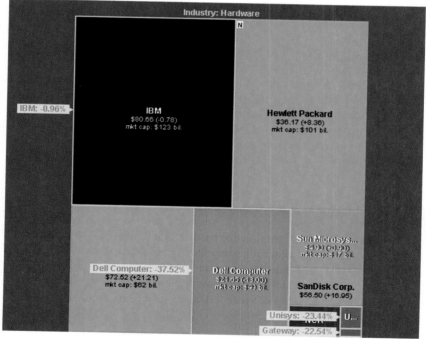

Fig. 5.24 Map of the Market shows the details for companies that deal with hardware. Image reproduced with the permission of ©SmartMoney.com.

minutes to allow the financial operator to check the entire stock market at a glance. Every colored rectangle of the map represents an individual company quoted on the stock market. The rectangle's size reflects the company's capitalization, which is the total market value of the shares issued by the company (in other words, the "big" companies are represented by rectangles of larger areas). The color reflects price performance in the period of time considered. In the example in Fig. 5.23, green means the stock price is up, red means it's down, dark colors indicate stationary situations, and the intensity of color reflects the importance of the variations. The user can get an idea of the entire stock market sector and compare different sectors and titles through the color of the blocks. The map is created by a Java applet, which the user can open with a browser connected to the website, and is very interactive. Using the appropriate controls, a user can see the details of every single title (for example, in Fig. 5.23, Dell Computer have been selected and present a strong negative variation over the last year), change the color scheme (particularly useful to color-blind people), change the time period of reference, or highlight the top five gainers or losers. Above all, the user can explore the map by zooming in on a particular sector or type of industry (the example in Fig. 5.24 represents the details of some companies that deal with computer hardware, indicating the shares with major losses).

5.2.5.3 SequoiaView

SequoiaView[9] and its clone applications, KDirStat for UNIX[10] and WinDirStat for Windows,[11] use treemaps to display the disk usage in terms of the dimension of files and folders. SequoiaView introduced a variant to treemaps: the *squarified cushion treemaps* [63] [6]. The screen is subdivided so that the rectangles resemble a square as closely as possible, to improve the readability of small files, which often leads to thin rectangles in the original treemap. Also, ridges are added to each rectangle. SequoiaView was developed by the Computer Science Department of the Technische Universiteit Eindhoven. A screenshot appears in Fig.5.25.

5.3 Conclusion

Several real-world datasets are organized other in the form of connections or containments, which can be naturally represented by graphs and trees. In these representations, items are encoded with nodes and relationships with edges. These types of representation are critical when there is a high number of nodes or edges: Crossing edges and overlapping nodes may make the visual representation unreadable.

---

[9] http://www.win.tue.nl/sequoiaview.

[10] http://kdirstat.sourceforge.net.

[11] http://windirstat.info.

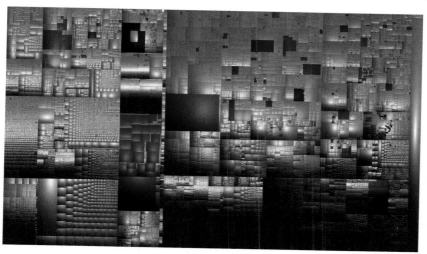

Fig. 5.25 Squarified cushion treemap in SequoiaView showing the whole content of the file system.

To reduce the complexity of a graph, one can intervene by attempting to diminish the number of nodes or edges visualized or using geometric node arrangements that improve readability or add interactivity. Trees are convenient way to represent hierarchical data. However, there are other ways to represent hierarchical data that allow to see their attributes and to identify specific patterns or properties of the hierarchy, such as the treemaps. In this chapter, we have shown some techniques that may help with the representation of complex graphs or trees.

Chapter 6
World Wide Web

In 1993, at the faculty of Computer Science at Pisa where I was a student, we abandoned the character terminals of the UNIX workstation to move on to the novelty of the year: the web browser. It was a revolution for everyone: Not only was e-mail and software exchange available through FTP, the Internet finally allowed everyone, at the same time, to download and visualize the first graphical and multimedia contents thanks to the web browsers. They were the times of Mosaic and HTML 1.0; the "Web" has come a long way since then. Conceived of as a tool for the exchange of information in a scientific environment, the Internet has become a mass medium where almost anything can be found. It is precisely this great quantity of information and data made available these days that has inspired some researchers to explore new visualization techniques specific to this type of media. Since it deals with data that belong to a particular website or the combined information of several websites, the visualization techniques can often prevent the "surfer" from getting lost in the sea of pages and links.

It is important to specify that the data relative to the websites fall into the typologies shown in the previous chapter (in particular, the pages of a website and their links have a network structure), but, in view of their specific solutions, we dedicate this chapter to their treatment.

6.1 Website Maps

The web-surfing population is very familiar with a document that is often present in websites: the *site map*. A newcomer to the Web would expect a real "map," meaning a visual representation, more or less detailed, of what is contained within the site. Instead, it almost always consists of a simple list of pages where, sometimes, a minimum of hierarchical structure is attempted. I have never fully understood the usefulness of this type of map, and I have always preferred a straightforward "search" tool to the maps listing the titles of the pages, which in fact are becoming less and less used in modern websites.

R. Mazza, *Introduction to Information Visualization*,
DOI: 10.1007/978-1-84800-219-7_6, © Springer-Verlag London Limited 2009

The actual concept of a "site map" is not mistaken and can be very useful for "guiding" visitors toward the page they are looking for. The typical questions that the website visitor asks when brought to a page through a link, perhaps by the results of a search engine, are the following: Where am I? What's in this website? The map is the instrument we use to get our bearings when we find ourselves in unfamiliar territory. It is important not to confuse a map with something else. We like to think of a map as such, and we believe that some solutions can be very valid.

Some companies have recognized the potentiality that these tools can offer for improving web communication, and have made maps their business. Such is the case of *Dynamic Diagrams*,[1] one of the leading companies in the production of maps and analysis tools for websites. This company, whose core business is "help people to understand information", has developed visual tools for designing and creating website maps. On the one hand, these maps can be used in the design phase (or revision) of website architecture and therefore turn out to be of use to those carrying out this phase; on the other hand, this technology may be used to create actual surfing maps for website users. Figure 6.1 shows a map that describes the main structure of a website (Nature Neuroscience), realized by Dynamic Diagrams to design the new site architecture. The map represents the hierarchical structure of the site, through a careful selection of graphical elements: The single pages are represented through "cards," as in the dominoes game; the various zones of the website are separated by the types of users who access it (subscriber, registered user, visitor) and are arranged on raised levels of different color-coded carpets; at the bottom right is the number of links on which the users have to click to reach a particular page, starting at the home page. An important characteristic of this map is the use of an isometric perspective view that maintains a uniform dimension for all of the objects laid out on an *isometric plan*. Usually, the three-dimensional views use a perspective projection that tends to represent the objects that are further away from the viewer in a smaller proportion with respect to the objects that are closer. Dynamic Diagrams specialists believe that an isometric projection, where objects are not distorted by mapping the 3D into a 2D view and have a constant scale across the space, is clearer and more legible for this type of map.

This type of view can also be used to create maps dedicated to website visitors. MAPA software is written in Java, realized by Dynamic Diagrams, that creates an interactive map of a website by analyzing the site's current structure. An example of a map created with this software is shown in Fig. 6.2, which represents the map of the Dynamic Diagrams website. The page cards, which represent the website pages, are arranged according to the hierarchical structure of the site, beginning from the current page, indicated by a red marker at the top (in the figure, it is the home page of the site), working toward the top right-hand corner of the figure. The colors mark different levels of the hierarchy, in order to have a visual idea of the position of a page in the navigational hierarchy of the site. The user can interact with the map in several ways. For instance, by placing the mouse pointer over a card, the title of the page is visualized; a double click directly opens the corresponding page on the

---

[1] http://www.dynamicdiagrams.com.

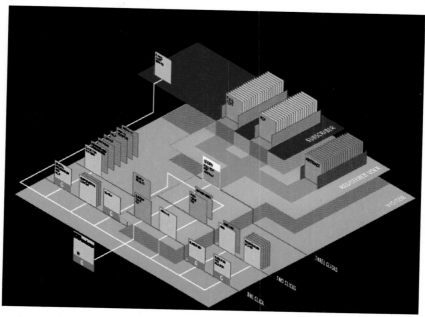

Fig. 6.1 Map of the structure of the Nature Neuroscience website realized by Dynamic Diagrams. Image reproduced with the permission of Dynamic Diagrams.

browser. In complex websites, one can choose to visualize only part of the structure. The user can click on the card with a dark bar at the top to reorganize the map and refocus the layout in relation to the selected page.

Besides describing the structure of a website, maps are also excellent tools for guiding users through the navigation of intricate websites. For example, Fig. 6.3 represents a navigational map used in an online course on verbal semiotics, held in the Department of Communication Sciences at the University of Lugano. The map uses an archipelago of islands to represent the course's topics. The students can click on the islands to have a more detailed map of the topic or to reach the materials for that topic. Students use the map to have an overview of the various topics, and it shows the reference points required for an orientation in studying various parts of the course.

6.2 Website Log Data

One of the functions performed by a web server is that of recording every request made by users who access the site with their browser; these requests are kept in a special text file, the *log file*, which memorizes the information that may be useful for statistical means and for controlling possible errors or unauthorized accesses to

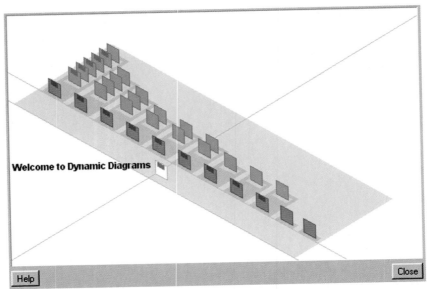

Fig. 6.2 Site map of the Dynamic Diagrams website. Image reproduced with the permission of Dynamic Diagrams.

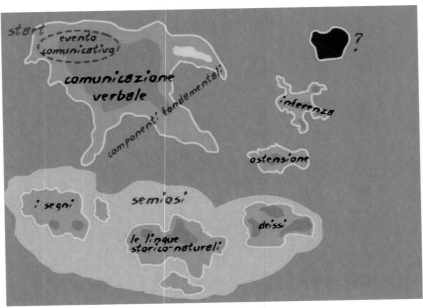

Fig. 6.3 Content map of an online course. Image reproduced with the permission of Andrea Rocci, University of Lugano.

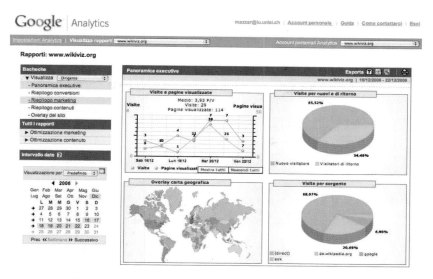

Fig. 6.4 Google^{TM} analytics. Image reproduced with the permission of Google^{TM}.

the website. Among the information memorized on the log file are the IP address of
the computer that has sent a request, the date and time of the request, the URL of the
requested file, the size of the requested file, the type of browser, and the operating
system used by the user. Besides the text, a web page can contain other elements,
such as images or animations. For instance, the images contained in the web pages
correspond to particular files and consequently a single request of a web page may
correspond to several entries in the log file.

If analyzed and interpreted correctly, log files can provide a useful source of
important information for the management and marketing of the website. To analyze
a log file, one uses programs that analyze and present the data memorized in the log
file, in a form comprehensible to the human reader. The use of these programs is
mainly directed at commercial motives; for example, webmasters are used to learn
the habits and surfing preferences of users who visit a website. The problems tackled
by this type of software and the types of data manipulated lend themselves well to
being treated in graphical form.

In business, there are dozens of software products to serve this purpose. The
types of visual representations usually used by commercial software are mainly histograms, line graphs, and pie charts. Figure 6.4 gives an example of a page generated
by the Google^{TM} "Analytics" tool. Each webmaster can create an account on Google
Analytics, insert a required Javascript code on a page of the website that he or she is
interested in monitoring, and Google Analytics records the data of users who access
that website. Google Analytics is particularly sophisticated as it provides a series of
preconfigured representations for different types of users.

The main problem of website analysis software is that users have difficulty
putting the data presented in graphs and pie charts in context with the website pages,

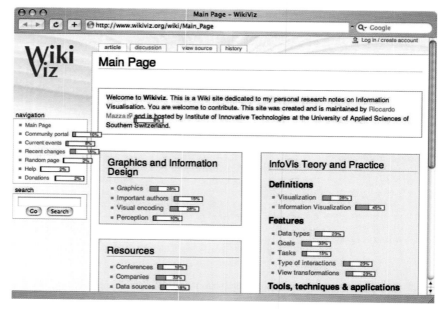

Fig. 6.5 Website statistics through an overlay representation.

and so alternative graphical forms have recently been researched. A solution adopted by a growing number of programs, is that of representing the statistical data directly on the site pages, so that the site manager understands to which link (and therefore which pages) the data processed by the log analysis software refers. This can be done by laying the values over the links present in the pages; this way we know, for example, what percentage of visitors to the site click on a particular link (see Fig. 6.5). This technique is called *overlay*, precisely from laying the analyzed values of the log file over the site pages.

Another very interesting aspect in the analysis of a site is understanding which path most of the users follow in navigating the website pages. This task is commonly called *path analysis*. How many visitors arrive at the home page and don't go on to visit any other pages? Which page is visited most frequently after the home page? What are users' entrance and exit pages of the website? Maybe a page that we deem to be very important and should be read by all isn't even considered in this path. All this information can be derived from navigation analysis and from the log file of the website. This type of analysis is very important for understanding how to optimize the general organization of a website. The problem, from a communication point of view, is always that of rendering the information explicit to the user in an effective and intuitive way. Also, in this case, diverse strategies of representation have been used, which go from a simple list, table, or histogram put in order based on the path, to more complex representations featuring graphs. Figure 6.6 shows a navigation graph of a website. Colors, labels, and geometric figures are used to help the interpretation of the graph. The "external" web pages are represented through

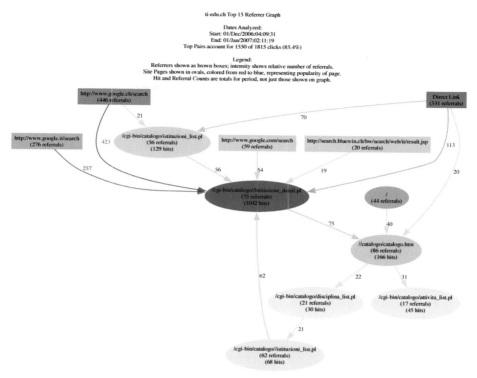

Fig. 6.6 Representation of the navigation of a website through a graph. Graph generated through the StatViz tool (http://statviz.sourceforge.net/).

brown rectangles, while the intensity of the color reflects the number of accesses to the site that come from these pages (*referrals*). The internal pages are represented through the red- to blue-colored ovals; also in this case, the color indicates the number of accesses to the pages, and therefore its level of popularity among visitors. The connections indicate the navigation path, while the labels on edges indicate the number of visitors to have browsed the site following that path.

The graph represented in Fig. 6.6 is certainly much more expressive than a simple table or histogram and very clearly indicates where the site visitors come from, which is the first page they access, and which pages are most frequently consulted successively. For example, it clearly appears that search engines bring the majority of visitors to access one particular dynamic page of the site (/cgi-bin/catalog/istituzione_detail.pl), while no one accesses the first page of the site (/) through an external referral.

6.3 Visual Representation of Search Engine Results

Search engines are the main tools for searching for information on the Internet. Some of these, like Google, are fed by agents (called *crawlers* or *robots*) that browse the World Wide Web continuously, in an automated manner, following links to discover new sites and update the references to contents of already-known pages. Others, like the Yahoo directory, are managed by human operators who keep an archive of websites structured through a set of hierarchical categories. From the viewpoint of precision and information quality, a directory like Yahoo, being managed by individuals and not crawlers, provides a better guarantee of the quality and relevance of the information. Unfortunately, today's websites are so numerous and so dynamic that no organization that manages directories manually can offer a guarantee of the completeness of catalogued sites. For this reason, the search engines that use crawler-driven information retrieval tools, like Google, are the foremost resource that people use when they need to search for information online.

All of the search engines work through a standard interaction model and a representation format of the results: The user inserts a search string that represents the topic of interest; the engine returns a series of results, each of which is represented by the page title, a link, and a concise description of the contents of the found page. It's a model that is, by now, consolidated in the habits of every Internet user. However, it is not rare to come across a search that returns thousands of results and, even worse, discover that a great number of those results have nothing to do with what the user was looking for.

Although this form of presentation of results has become the de facto standard of every search engine, other types of visual representation have been explored. Those that make use of representation forms that users are familiar with, like the scatterplot and the bar graph, seem the most promising. This is precisely the type of approach followed by a group of researchers directed by Harald Reiterer of the University of Konstanz in Germany, which has produced the INSYDER tool [49]. INSYDER offers diverse ways to present the results of an Internet search; besides the classic textual ranked list, other graphical interfaces are offered to help the user in the information search process (see Fig. 6.7).

The documents that constitute search results can be represented by elements in a 2D scatterplot (Fig. 6.7, top) that maps a predefined number of attributes onto the x- and y- axes:

- date/relevance,
- server type/number of documents,
- relevance/server type.

This way the user's attention can focus on documents published after a certain date, as well as a certain level of relevance. The server type of the document determines the source (URL) of a document, useful when the user needs to see at a glance what kind of source the document is coming from. For instance, business decision makers can use a server type definition containing the name of competitors; in this way, the user can determine at once if the document is from a competitor,

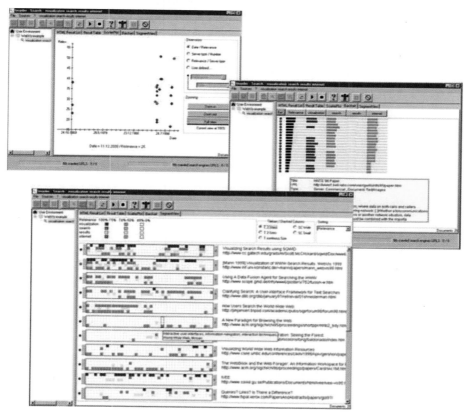

Fig. 6.7 INSYDER graphical interface for the visualization of search engine results: *scatterplot* (top), *bar graph* (center), and *tile bar* (bottom). Image published on [49] and reproduced with the permission of Harald Reiterer, University of Konstanz; ©Springer-Verlag 2005.

without paying attention to the URL of documents. Another interface makes use of a bar graph (Fig. 6.7, center) to show the level of relevance of each term in every document. A search can, in fact, be specified through a number of terms, called *keywords*. For example, inserting the string: "hotel Lugano view lake" specifies a search looking for the documents that contain these four keywords (hotel + Lugano + view + lake). Each row of the graph represents a document and each column represents the distribution of the relevance for each single keyword in that document, while the overall relevance is shown in the first black column of the visual representation. This way, it is simple and immediate to detect if a document deals with one or more of the di?erent keywords of the query. A further visual representation, called *tile bar* (Fig. 6.7, bottom), is provided to carry out a detailed analysis of the structure on single documents. In this case, each document is represented through a rectangular bar subdivided into rows that correspond to the keywords of the query. The length of the rectangle indicates the length of the document. The bar is also subdivided into columns, each column referring to a segment within the document. For each segment, the cell corresponding to every keyword is colored with an intensity reflecting the relevance of the concept for that segment of the document. The darker the color of the cell, the higher the relevance. A white cell indicates no relevance for the keyword. With this interface the user is offered the possibility to rate, as precisely as possible, the degree of relevance in every section of a document: Documents that have an high number of sections having overlapping colored cells are more likely to be relevant than others that instead have a much more fragmented situation.

6.3.1 Clustering

New approaches to the search for information on the internet try to "impose" their identity for a more natural representation of the relationships between websites and documents in the network. Among the most interesting examples there are the search engines that provide *clusters* of results. Instead of presenting a long list with thousands of results, clustering-based search engines analyze the contents of the pages found and try to extract the main topics, which are then used to group similar results together into cluster. For example, performing a search on Google with the term "Lugano" currently returns a list of over 11 million results—certainly, too many to be taken into consideration by any surfer. Trying to carry out the same search with the most prominent cluster search engine, *Clusty*, (http://www.clusty.com) we do still attain a huge number of results, but Clusty also presents us with a cluster organization of the most characteristic terms and clusters a large part of the results. For instance, searching for the term "Lugano" with Clusty, we are offered the following clusters[2]: Hotel, Lake Lugano, Ticino, Photos, Tourism, University, Lake, Club, and Museum and Art. The user can click on one of these terms and consult the websites and pages that deal specifically with each one. Searches of this type can be very useful when the user has a very vague idea of what to search for. For example, through the "Museum and Art" cluster, we immediately find out about a certain number of sites that describe the Lugano Museum of Modern Art, information that we might have only found by surfing beyond the third or fourth page of results with other, more traditional, search engines.

Some search engines try to represent the clusters generated by the search algorithms through maps. One of these is KartOO (http://www.kartoo.com), which positions the most relevant sites in the center of an interactive map. Figure 6.8 represents the results of a search in which the term "Lugano" is specified as the search string. The most relevant sites (meaning those that have had the highest "ranking" in the search) are positioned at the center of the figure and correspond to the sites of the tourist office of the region (http://www.lugano-tourism.ch) and the institutional portal of the Lugano council (http://www.lugano.ch). The clusters (called *topics*) de-

---

[2] Search performed February 19, 2007.

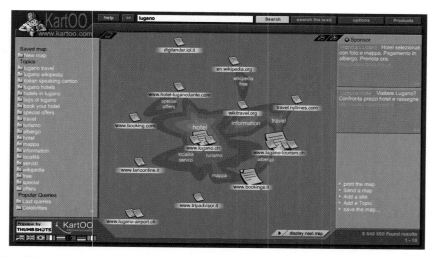

Fig. 6.8 Results of the web search using KartOO. Image reproduced with the permission of KartOO SA.

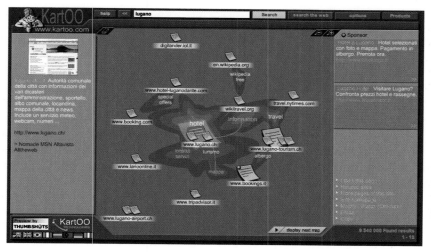

Fig. 6.9 Selection of the www.lugano.ch website in the KartOO search interface. Image reproduced with the permission of KartOO SA.

termined by the search are listed in the frame on the left, shown in a purely textual form. It is worth mentioning that the most important clusters are also reported in the map in the form of "islands." The user can position the mouse pointer over one of these terms to see which sites, among those reported on the map, belong to the cluster; alternatively, the user can position the mouse pointer over one of the sites to find out which cluster it is part of and to see a preview of the site in the frame on the left (see Fig. 6.9).

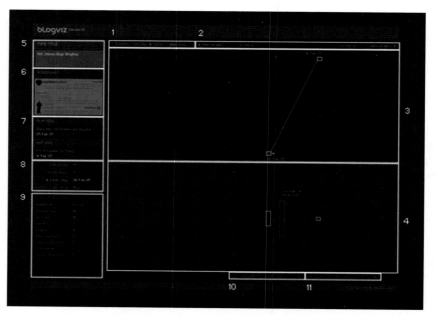

Fig. 6.10 Blogviz graphical interface. Images reproduced with the permission of Manuel Lima.

6.4 Analysis of Interactions in Blogs

The "social web", also known as *Web 2.0*, refers to the relatively recent phenomena of web sites that are predominantly populated by user generated content. Wiki, blog, tagging, sharing, folksonomies, ... are just some of the terms used in websites that aim to enhance creativity, information sharing, collaboration, and connectivity among users. In particular, blogs presents one of the most interesting social phenomenons of our time. With this tool anyone can provide comments, opinions, or news on a particular subject. Thanks to blogs, the opinions of unknown people have been read by thousands of people worldwide. Some blogs have become so famous as to constitute a reference point for topics such as politics, sport, and culture. Recently, some sites have been founded, like Technorati (http://technorati.com), with which one can search for blogs that deal with a specific topic.

The dynamic of the blog community is the subject of study of many scholars; an experimental tool, blogviz,[3] has been developed to facilitate the analysis of how discussions on a particular topic are developed within blogs. This tool proposes a modality of visual analysis of how the discussions on a topic evolve in a certain number of blogs. The prototype, developed by Manuel Lima as part of his master's thesis, analyzes the discussions that took place in 444 blogs during the first 64 days of 2005. In these blogs, 12 topics were monitored; each topic can be singled

---

[3] http://www.blogviz.com.

out graphically in the cross-sectional lines represented in frame no. 3 in Fig. 6.10. This frame has two time scales, positioned at the top and bottom. Every topic of discussion is represented by a line that connects the first day in which the topic is discussed (bottom scale) with the last day of discussion (top). The width of the line represents the number of blogs in which the topic is discussed. In the bottom frame (no. 4), a bar graph shows, each day, how many blogs have discussed the topic. The goal of this visualization is to study how the discussion of a topic evolves over time. In frame no. 3, in particular, the slope of the line is indicative of the duration of the discussion: the higher the inclination, the briefer the discussion period. In addition, the tool offers further useful information for the study of blogs, such as the first and last blogs that discussed the topic and the list of the bloggers who were most active in proposing new topics for discussion. Unfortunately, blogviz remained a prototype and was never launched as a production tool.

6.5 Conclusion

In this chapter, we have dealt with data that we run into in numerous and varied situations: data from the World Wide Web. Web pages, sites, links, maps, and clusters are examples of multidimensional data that we come across when we browse the Web and, because of their complex and extensive nature, sometimes create the "lost in space" syndrome of the Web surfer. For this reason, we have proposed some visual representations in this chapter, to help the user (or the website manager) deal with this huge amount of information. Far from being fully explored, this area of research is one of the most active and, probably, the most promising in providing new insightful visualizations.

Chapter 7
Interactions

In the previous chapters, we looked at some visual representations with which the user can interact to modify the general view. For example, in a three-dimensional view, the user may rotate the image, to be able to reveal rear objects that could otherwise be occluded by others in the foreground. Basically, actions like geometric transformations of the view, filtering the input data, or even changing the type of representation allow the user to make the best of the visual representations; sometimes this is fundamental to carrying out explorative analysis on a collection of data. In this chapter, we'll take a closer look at the mechanism of interaction and show how this can be useful with numerous practical examples.

7.1 The Problem of Information Overload

In the book's introduction, we touched on how the quantity of information to be processed has grown to such a high level over the past decade that by now we just can't do without computers, handhelds, cell phones, and anything else that can be used not only for communicating with others, but also for memorizing and organizing our ideas, information, photos, letters, reports, etc. Information visualization seeks to meet the needs of those users who, with computers, make use of graphical interfaces that take advantage of humans' notable perceptual ability of vision systems for visually exploring data at various levels of abstraction. In the previous chapters, we reviewed some techniques that can be useful for representing certain data types and meet specific user goals. Unfortunately, all of the techniques encounter the same physical problem when a certain amount of data is exceeded: the lack of space for representing all of the data intended for visualization.

Interactive tools can come to our aid. In particular, information visualization systems appear to be most useful when a user can modify the input data, change the visual mapping, or manipulate the view generated. Interactions facilitate data exploration and may uncover relationships that could remain hidden in a static view. The techniques that we are going to examine, regardless of their simplicity or sophistica-

R. Mazza, *Introduction to Information Visualization*,
DOI: 10.1007/978-1-84800-219-7_7, © Springer-Verlag London Limited 2009

tion, have a common objective: that of providing a global overview of the collection of data and, at the same time, letting users analyse specific details or parts that they may judge as relevant to their goal.

In 1996 Ben Shneiderman wrote an article [52] that defined, for the first time, a taxonomy of the possible tasks one may achieve with the graphical interfaces that make use of visual representations. The article became famous among researchers who deal with this discipline, thanks to a guideline, genial in its simplicity, of designing a interactive information visualization system, defined by Shneiderman as the "information visualization's mantra":[1]

> First, **overview**,
> then, **zoom** and **filtering**,
> finally, **details on demand**.

The mantra clearly indicates how an information visualization system can support users in the process of searching for information. It is necessary to provide a global overview of the entire collection of data, so that users gain an understanding of the entire dataset, than users may filter the data to focus on a specific part of particular interest. Finally, all the details of a particular instance of data ought to be visible, should the user require them.

7.2 Types of Interactive Visual Representations

In Chapter 2, we saw a model of the visualization process, which allows the user to intervene at every stage of the process (Fig. 2.1). Depending on the type of interaction a user can perform, we can specify the following types of representation:

- **Static representations** don't allow users to perform any type of interaction, and only a single, unmodifiable view is generated.
- **Manipulable representations** allow users to manipulate the process that generates the view, via zooming, rotation, panning, etc.
- **Transformable representations** allow users to manipulate, in the preprocessing phase, the input data of the representations, for example through data filtering. These manipulations usually influence and modify the images that are generated.

In the following sections, we will examine some of the most interesting techniques for the manipulation and transformation of visual representations.

---

[1] The mantra is a form of spiritual practice, used in some religions, involving the continuous repetition of a word or certain number of phrases, with the aim of attaining a particular effect on a mental level. The most well-known mantra is the *Om* mantra practiced in Buddhism.

7.3 Manipulable Representations

A process of interactive visual representation can be defined as *manipulable* when the user can intervene and manipulate the view generated. The most common techniques apply geometric transformations, such as zooming onto a particular part of the view or rotating an image in a three-dimensional view. There are several techniques for view manipulation other than zooming and rotation; the most popular can be grouped into three categories:

- scrolling,
- overview + details,
- focus + context.

We are about to examine each of these categories.

7.3.1 Scrolling

Scrolling is a very common technique that we regularly use when working with a computer. It consists of visualizing only the part of the view that can be contained in the physical area on the screen and, through appropriate movement bars called *scrollbars*, allows the user to move the visible parts. This technique has the advantage of being acquired and consolidated in all of the basic window systems but has a defect of hiding the global vision of the entire view, which can be a problem when there is a need to contextualize the visual part within the entire collection of data.

7.3.2 Overview + Details

The basic idea of the *overview + details* technique is to show a detailed part of the view on the screen (exactly as scrolling does) while providing an global, less detailed, view of the entire representation. The name is derived from this approach, which shows the overall structure of the content to help users make first impressions, and understand how the entire collection is organized. The details, on the other hand, let the user "drill down" from that view into the details as they need to, keeping both levels visible for quick iteration. We show an example of this technique in Fig. 7.1, in which the details of a graph are visualized in the window, which maintains an overview in a window in the top right corner with an indication of the area represented in detail. Through zooming and panning operations, the user can widen or narrow the area visualized in detail and move (by operating the mouse on the rectangle with the red borders) the zone that displays the details.

This technique is applied in some applications that use the magnifying glass metaphor to show the details of a zone of the view. In the Microsoft Windows characters map (Fig. 7.2), for instance, the user can see an enlarged view of each letter

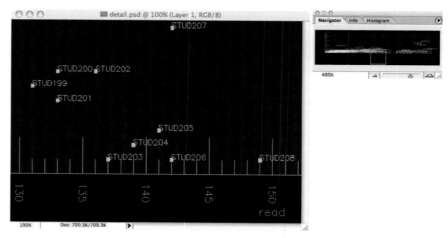

Fig. 7.1 Example of the application of the Overview + Details technique.

by passing the mouse pointer over a character, allowing the user to easily distinguish it among the other characters in a very contained space.

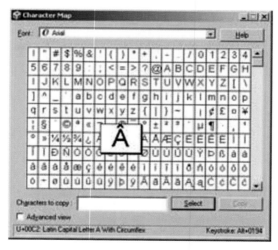

Fig. 7.2 Map of the characters used by Microsoft Windows to assist the user in the choice of a special character. © Microsoft.

The magnifying glass metaphor are best applied in applications that require the maximization of space for the overview portion. Figure 7.3 illustrates an application that shows a tourist map of Florence. To dedicate all of the available space to the visualization of the map, an appropriate lens can be placed over the map and moved by using the mouse. When the lens is placed over a building of touristic interest, a

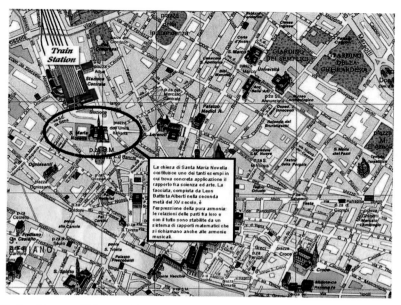

Fig. 7.3 Tourist map of Florence. By moving the lens over the building of touristic interest, it is possible to see an area in which the details of the building are illustrated.

small section of text becomes visible featuring a detailed description of the selected building.

Other examples of applications that use the overview + details technique are the *zoomable user interfaces* (ZUIs), which use zooming as the main method for exploring items of information that are too numerous to be displayed on a single screen. ZUIs have been investigated for several years at the *Human–Computer Interaction Lab* (HCIL) of the University of Maryland, which has also made two toolkits for building such interfaces available, Jazz and Piccolo[2] [3, 2]. The ZUIs display the graphical representation on a virtual desktop instead of in a window. The virtual desktop is rather wide and has a very high resolution. A portion of this huge virtual desktop is seen on the display through a virtual camera that the user can pan across the surface in two dimensions, and smoothly zoom into objects of interest, for more detailed information, and zoom out for an overview.

An example of an application developed using the Piccolo ZUI toolkit is Pho-toMesa,[3] a zoomable image browser. It provides a zoomable environment for users to view the images contained in multiple directories of the computer, and allows users to surf and browse through simple navigational commands to smoothly zoom in and out (see a screenshot in Fig. 7.4).

---

[2] http://www.cs.umd.edu/hcil/piccolo.

[3] http://www.windsorinterfaces.com/photomesa.shtml.

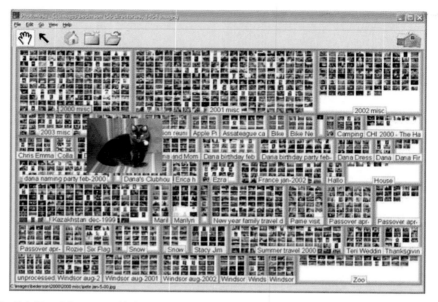

Fig. 7.4 PhotoMesa zoomable image browser. Image reproduced with the permission of Ben Bederson, Windsor Interfaces, Inc.

More recently, Apple adopted a similar interaction modality in the user interface of the iPhone, which enables the user to zoom in and out of web pages and photos by placing two fingers on the screen and sliding them farther apart or closer together.

7.3.3 Focus + Context

Another family of view manipulation techniques is called *focus + context*. This consists of simultaneously providing the user with detailed (focus) and contextual (context) information in the same area, without using two separate views. The goal is to dedicate the whole space in the screen to the detailed view, which is what interests the user but, at the same time, it strives to retain the context within which the details are positioned. This can be done either through the distortion of the view or through the elimination of the details in the peripheral zones.

The distortion techniques literally create a distortion of the image generated by the view, to dedicate a large part of the screen to the details of interest to the user. Some notable works, which we find very often in literature, are the *bifocal views*, the *perspective wall*, and the *fisheye view*, whereas *hyperbolic browser* and *SpaceTree* use a technique that eliminates the details of the peripheral zone.

7.3.3.1 Bifocal View

Over the last 15 years, the technology of computer monitors and displays has evolved (although not at the same frenzied speed as other computer components, such as the processor and memory). In fact, in the early 1990s, the most common monitor resolution was 640×480 pixels; today it is possible to avail of monitors with a 1600×1200 pixels resolution at a reasonable cost. However, despite this increase in the number of pixels and, consequently, the visible area, the available space is not always sufficient for containing more complex representations.

Robert Spence, as far back as 1982, was the first to propose a solution by means of a view distortion technique [53]. If an image is too large to be visualized in the computer screen, then a distorted vision can be provided to contain it in the visible area of the screen. The problem, however, is how and in what way to apply the distortion.

As we have mentioned many times, every visual representation should allow the user to observe the details of a part of the view and, at the same time, retain an idea of the global view. Following this principle, distortion techniques combine a part of the screen (central) in which the detailed information (the *focus*) is presented and the peripheral parts are distorted (through a transformation function), allowing the image to be contained in the screen and simultaneously providing the context in which the detail is placed (the *context*). In particular, the *bifocal display* applies a transformation outside the two vertical axes, as shown in Fig. 7.5.

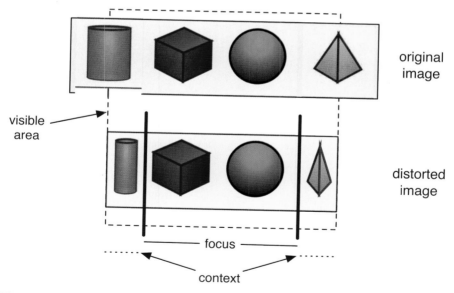

Fig. 7.5 Bifocal display.

7.3.3.2 Perspective Wall

The *perspective wall* [40] is an application derived from the bifocal display, but it uses a three-dimensional perspective for the context. The front wall is used to display the focus of the data while the two side walls show contextual information with a decreasing magnification level from the front wall (see Fig. 7.6). This intuitive distortion of the layout provides efficient use of screen space. The technique was developed at the Xerox Palo Alto Research Center and is currently used by Business Objects[4] (the same company that produces TableLens) for *TimeWall* software. Further mapping on the space has been added to the perspective wall. For example, in Fig. 7.6, the icons represent movies, arranged horizontally in chronological order and vertically by distributors. Color is used to distinguish the genre (action, comedy, drama, etc.). In this case, we assume that the users are particularly interested in the release date and the distributor of the movie.

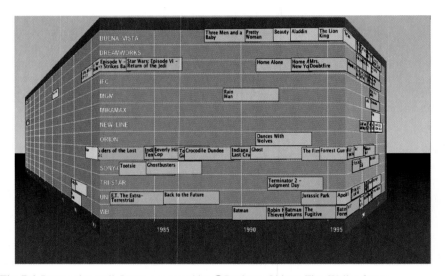

Fig. 7.6 Perspective wall. Image generated by ©Business Objects TimeWall software.

7.3.3.3 Fisheye View

Created from a proposal by George Furnas, the *fisheye view* [23] introduces a visualization technique of the focus + context type, inspired by the human visual system. When observing an object, the human visual system simultaneously perceives the

---

[4] Business Objects S.A. is a global business intelligence (BI) software company recently acquired by SAP AG. In 2007, Business Objects acquired Inxight Software, the original producer of Table-Lens and TimeWall software. http://www.businessobjects.com.

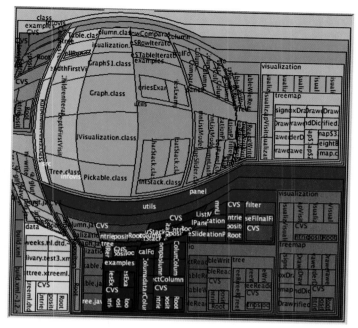

Fig. 7.7 Fisheye distorted treemap.

object itself and the immediate nearby area. We focus on a particular zone, but the area surrounding remains perceptible to our attention, with a detail that fades increasingly the further it gets from the image's focal point. The basic principle of this technique is precisely that of representing the most relevant information in a focal point, with the maximum detail, while the peripheral information is presented with lesser detail. A level of relevance is defined for each element; it is calculated on the importance of the information and its distance from the center of the focus. Figure 7.7 shows a treemap in which a fisheye distortion has been applied through a magnifying glass-type effect.

Researchers have tried to maximize the use of this technique in all ways, proposing its use in numerous contexts. One of these is the *fisheye menus*, defined at the HCIL Lab at the University of Maryland [1]. The goal of this application is to facilitate the user in choosing options presented through drop-down menus, which are ubiquitous in all graphical user interfaces. The fisheye menus dynamically change the dimension of the font of the drop-down menu, so that the elements near the cursor appear in a normal font, while the other, distant elements still remain visible, but with a font size that decreases gradually the farther the element is from the cursor. Figure 7.8 gives an example that requires the user to choose among 256 nations represented in the menu. The version on the left presents a normal drop-down menu, while that on the right is a version realized with a fisheye view. The researchers who created this type of menu hope for widespread use in commercial applications.

Fig. 7.8 Example of a drop-down menu with scrollbar (left) and the fisheye version (right). Image reproduced with the permission of Ben Bederson, University of Maryland, Human–Computer Interaction Lab.

However, the common drop-down menu is consolidated in almost any graphical interface, and the difficulty of using the lens of the fisheye version (in fact, a small movement of the mouse provokes a notable change to elements in the focus) makes its adoption in commonly used interfaces very challenging.

7.3.3.4 Hyperbolic browser

Another focus + context type application that has become "historical" was developed by researchers of the Xerox PARC Lab at the beginning of the 1990s and is called *hyperbolic browser* (also known as *hyperbolic tree*) [37]. It deals with an interactive technique that aims to represent data structures of very large trees. Currently, this technique is used in the *StarTree* software, produced by Business Objects.

The root node is initially represented at the center of the image, while the child nodes are positioned in a radial arrangement, with lesser detail. Peripheral nodes are also displayed in an oval region, to a level of detail that still provides the context of the central node (see the example in Fig. 7.9). The interesting aspect is that the user can explore the tree by clicking on the nodes and moving them with the mouse.

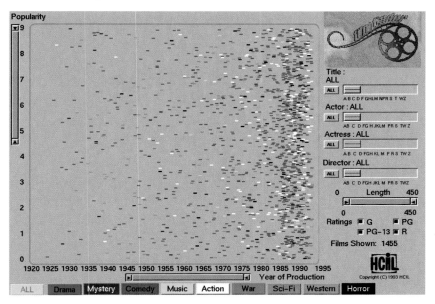

Fig. 7.11 A collective view of all of the available films in FilmFinder. Image reproduced with the permission of Ben Shneiderman, University of Maryland, Human–Computer Interaction Lab.

the film selected, including an image. It is interesting to note how the interaction approach adopted by FilmFinder (overview, filtering, and detail) corresponds to the indications of the *mantra* recommended by Ben Shneiderman.

7.4.4 Magic Lens

Conceived at the famous Xerox PARC Laboratory, the *magic lens* also constitutes an alternative approach to the dynamic query, which is offered to the user through the metaphor of an "intelligent" lens placed over a visual representation [21]. In a common 2D visual representation, such as a scatterplot, two attributes can be mapped onto the axes, while it is necessary to introduce other mapping, such as to color or shapes, to represent further attributes. When there are several attributes, the magic lens can be very helpful, as it extends the scatterplots or other similar 2D representations without sacrificing their simplicity. Basically, it consists of placing a lens (a movable shaped region) over a graphical representation, that affects the appearance of structures viewed through it. The operation performed by the lens is usually a filtering on the data viewed through the lens. An example appears in Fig. 7.14. The user can make a choice on which attribute to perform the filtering on and which operation to apply (by using the buttons on the right) and can set the threshold for the filter (by adjusting the cursor placed over the lens). The graphical elements

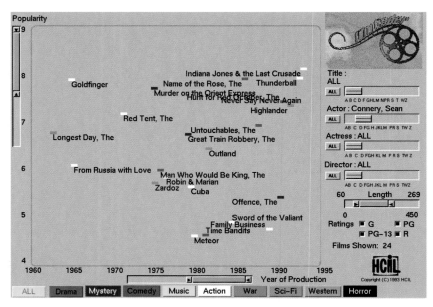

Fig. 7.12 Films listed after the filtering operation in FilmFinder. Image reproduced with the permission of Ben Shneiderman, University of Maryland, Human–Computer Interaction Lab.

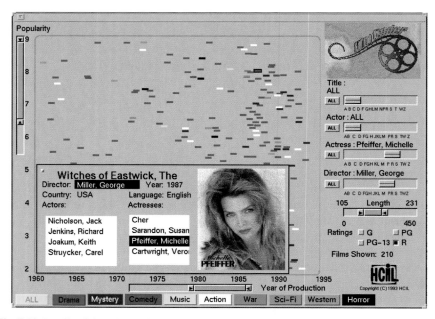

Fig. 7.13 Details of the selected film in FilmFinder. Image reproduced with the permission of Ben Shneiderman, University of Maryland, Human–Computer Interaction Lab.

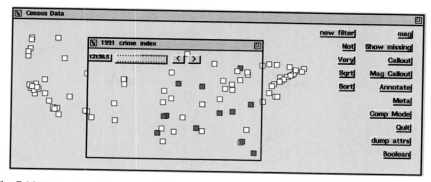

Fig. 7.14 Magic lens allows visual filtering of data in a scatterplot. Image reproduced with the permission of Eric Bier, Xerox PARC.

below the lens will change color according to the value of the filtered attribute. By placing overlapping lenses, one can carry out compositions of operations on more than one attribute.

7.4.5 Attribute Explorer

A further approach to formulate dynamic queries is represented by a system designed by Bob Spence's group in London in 1994 [62]. It uses cursors and histograms to explore the visual representations of a dataset's attributes. Each attribute to be explored is displayed as a histogram, with the range of attribute values segmented along the horizontal axis, and each data point displayed as a "stacked block" within its segment. The blocks in different histograms corresponding to values of a particular instance of the dataset are linked in a way that if the user filters the attribute values in one histogram, this filtering operation is reflected in other histograms as well.

Let's suppose that the dataset to graphically represent contains a number of real estate properties for sale. The properties are characterized by numerous attributes: number of rooms, square meters, age of the property, presence of a yard, and number of bathrooms, to mention just a few. This type of information is best treated with a graphical approach in that often, people, who wish to buy real estate have a very vague idea of what they want to buy. Buyers prefer to be fully understanding of what is available before making a decision on which house to visit for a possible purchase.

Let's suppose we have a dataset such as that reported in the following table:

Ref. N°	m²	Rooms	Price	Baths	Age
234a	85	3	320,000	1	12
29b	120	4	400,000	2	0
266r	75	2	270,000	1	5
322u	93	3	350,000	1	15
211e	110	4	380,000	1	12
209f	80	3	300,000	1	4
188a	80	3	280,000	1	0
190v	92	3	250,000	1	25

The attribute explorer representation is made up of a collection of five histograms, one for each dependent attribute listed in the previous table (Ref. N° is considered an independent attribute). For simplicity, Fig. 7.15 shows only the histograms relative to the "m²" (square meters), "Price," "Rooms," and "Baths" attributes. The histogram already provides an idea of the distribution of the values in the scale. We notice, for instance, that three properties have about 80 square meters (as there are three stacked blocks for this value). However, the most interesting aspect of this type of representation consists of

1. allowing the user to filter the values of one or more attributes, by moving the cursor located at the bottom to correspond with the histogram's axes (the color of the blocks changes according to the filtered value, where white indicates that the property meets the applied constraint),
2. linking the histograms of the various attributes, so that the filtering on an attribute is automatically reported in the other histograms as well.

In Fig. 7.15, we can notice that the block of the property having reference number 322u is gray, since we have filtered out properties with a price superior to 300,000 in the histogram on price. The same block, corresponding to property 322u, is colored gray in the other histograms also. This way we have an insight on how many (and which) properties satisfy the filtering on price in terms of square meters, rooms, and baths.

When filtering is applied to multiple attributes simultaneously, we can use the color intensity of blocks to encode how many attributes meet the applied constraint. For instance, we can use a progressively darker shade as attributes fail more constraints.

For a better understanding of attribute explorer, we recommend watching the Bob Spence video.[6]

7.5 Conclusion

In this chapter, we have dealt with interactive visual representations, which we have divided into manipulable and transformable representations. The former allows the

---
[6] Bob Spence's videos are available at http://www.iis.ee.ic.ac.uk/~r.spence/videos.htm.

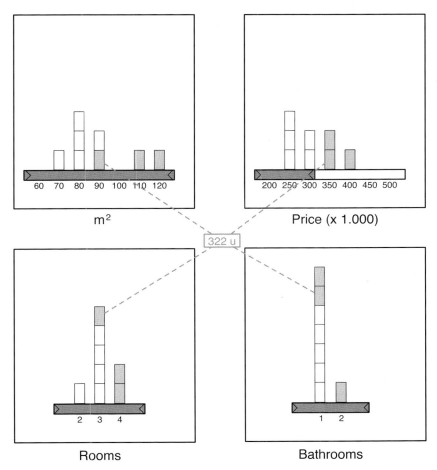

Fig. 7.15 In attribute explorer, the users can filter the values of one or more attributes by moving the cursors; the filtering on an attribute is automatically reported in the other histograms as well.

user to manipulate the view, while the latter allows the user to manipulate the source data and the mapping process. Both are very helpful in the process of explorative analysis, as they facilitate data exploration in large datasets and allow the user to get insights from the data.

Chapter 8
Evaluations

Systems that employ visual representations of information are thought of as being used by a particular category of users who have to carry out a specific task in a determined context. It is therefore a good idea to evaluate how these systems affect their users. An evaluation should provide the designer of an application with the data essential for understanding if, and under what conditions, it satisfies the users' needs, if it responds to their expectations and if users can effectively draw some benefit from the activity. A serious and rigorous evaluation is essential in the development process of a system that uses visual representations. Unfortunately, very often assessment is only marginally considered or even omitted. We believe, however, that the assessment of this type of system is of fundamental importance. A correct evaluation with the final users of the system can reveal potential problems and indicate which actions must be carried out to improve the quality. For this reason, we have dedicated an entire chapter to this, too often neglected, activity.

8.1 Human–Computer Interaction

Those who create systems that use visual representations, just like anyone who creates any type of software that presents a user interface, have to answer to the users of their own application sooner or later. At the beginning of the 1980s, when the first personal computers began to circulate outside universities and military research laboratories, the software available required a considerable level of competence to use. The user interfaces were complicated, as very few reflected humans communication methods, but, above all, because of the little care given to the aspect of user interaction. Interfaces of the early software constrained the users to adapt to the system, rather than having the system to adapt to the operating mode of the users.

The problem became evident primarily when the software started to be used by regular people, and not only by the professionals in the data centers. To study the problem from a scientific point of view, a discipline called *Human–Computer Inter-*

R. Mazza, *Introduction to Information Visualization*,
DOI: 10.1007/978-1-84800-219-7_8, © Springer-Verlag London Limited 2009

action (HCI) came about in the 1980s. This discipline uses analytic and empirical techniques to evaluate the effects of user interaction with computers.

A typical process of evaluation of a system in HCI usually has the following objectives [16]:

- *to assess the functionality of the system*, which means verifying that the system fulfills all of the functions requested by the user and defined in the phase of user requirements specification;
- *to analyze the effects of the system on the final users*, through a methodology that evaluates the aspects linked to the human factors, such as usability of the graphical interface, simplicity, and level of acceptance by the users;
- *to identify every possible problem that could arise with the final users of the system*, such as preventing an unpredicted result or anything that could be misleading to the users.

The evaluation of a system can be carried out during the design phase of an application or with a functional prototype. In the first case, we speak of *formative evaluation*, directed at identifying potential problems and indicating how to possibly improve the system design. In the second case, we speak of *summative evaluation*, which is often carried out with a sample of final users using a prototype of the system, to identify possible improvements to be applied in the final version of the system.

8.2 Evaluation Criteria

Engineering's best practices teach us that, before realizing any artifact, it's necessary to have performed a minimum of rational design of the system to be produced. This principle is valid in many disciplines: Before building a bridge, the engineer has to plan carefully, performing all the static and dynamic calculations to avoid having the bridge collapse when cars cross or in the presence of wind. Luckily, the design of a visual representation is not as critical as the building of a bridge. It is precisely this that causes many programmers to develop a visual representation without even the minimum of preliminary design. But, to avoid wasting time (and money), rigorous planning is essential for a successful project.

In the case of applications based on visual representations, two phases are very important: the specification of the requirements and the evaluation. All serious projects should start with a rigorous specification of the requirements, collected from potential users of the system through interviews, questionnaires, etc. Before starting a project, it is necessary to know your goals. Even the evaluation has to be carefully planned, and in the project phase we should have also plan the evaluation strategy. The evaluation should at least consider whether the product meets the specific requirements of the users, but that alone is not sufficient: The product must be effective and efficient and serve a purpose before it will be adopted by the final user.

Let's suppose, for example, that we have to evaluate the visual representation of data collected in a discussion forum, a representation that we implemented in Section 2.1 and is shown in Fig. 2.6. For this representation we could define an analysis in which the following criteria are evaluated:

Functionality. Does the visual representation provide all of the functionalities requested by the instructors and identified during the requirements elicitation?

Effectiveness. Does the visual representation provide the instructors with a better knowledge of the number of messages read and written in a discussion forum than the traditional interfaces provided by the tool? In particular, does the use of visual representations allow the instructors to have information on the number of messages sent and read with better accuracy and precision than other tools? Or, is there additional information that is made available exclusively by the visual representations?

Efficiency. Can the visual representation provide the instructors with information more rapidly than the tools provided by the system?

Usability. Is the interaction with the graphical interface simple and intuitive enough for the instructors?

Usefulness. In what way, and in what context, is the information provided by the graphical representation useful to the instructors?

The criteria just listed are the main objects of study in an evaluation process. However, depending on the type of application, and to limit the resources dedicated to the evaluation (which can be very long and expensive), one can limit the evaluation to only a subset of this criteria. For example, in some contexts it can be appropriate to evaluate the functionality, usability, and effectiveness of a representation, assuming that the usefulness is intrinsically derived from the new functionalities provided by the system and that the efficiency is not a critical factor to success. In the following sections, we will see some techniques in which the above-mentioned criteria can be evaluated.

8.3 Evaluating Visual Representations

The evaluation of systems that make use of visual representations, just like other systems involving direct interaction with humans, is an extremely complex task. In particular, it is very difficult to create an evaluation model that gives an objective judgment of the effectiveness and usefulness of a certain type of visualization. Two users placed in front of the same visual representation could express completely different and contrasting judgments. Experience, prior knowledge, and perceptive and cognitive ability may differ from person to person, which can bring about discord in judgment.

Chaomei Chen on his inspiring article on top 10 unsolved information visualization problems [9] put as the first three problems issues related to human factors (namely: usability issues, understanding elementary perceptual-cognitive tasks, prior knowledge), highlighting that there is still a lot of work to do on defining evaluation methods that involve real users and perceptual-cognitive tasks.

Diferent from a common user interface, a system that uses visual representations must be evaluated not only in terms of the usability and effectiveness of the interface, but also for the information that it manages to communicate to the users through perceptual and cognitive processes. For example, a crucial aspect could be to comprehend if users manage to decode the graphically codified information, if they can recognize visual patterns, if they manage to identify "interesting" values and elements, etc.

Not having their own evaluation methodology, systems that use visual representations have adopted techniques from human–computer interaction. These techniques, which have been in use for years, can essentially be subdivided into two categories: analytic evaluations and empirical evaluations.

8.3.1 Analytic Methods

Analytic evaluation methods come from psychological models of human–machine interaction and are mainly based on cognitive and behavioral studies. This type of evaluation is carried out by experts who verify whether a certain system is compliant with a series of principles called *heuristics* (from which the name *heuristic evaluation* originates). For example, some heuristics have been defined on the principles of the usability and accessibility of the graphical interface for common use applications. An evaluator use the system and judge its compliance with the heuristics.

Another type of test carried out by experts is called a *cognitive walkthrough*: An evaluator defines a series of possible *scenarios* of use and simulates the behavior of a user who uses the system to perform predetermined tasks. During the use, the evaluator has to identify possible problems that could originate from every task.

These types of evaluations are often used to judge the usability of the interfaces of the software systems, particularly in the initial phases of development, to identify possible problems and indicate modifications to improve the aspect of the interaction with the user. However, because of the difficulty in defining a series of heuristics for visual representations, these techniques are rarely adopted in information visualization.

8.3.2 Empirical Methods

Empirical evaluation methods make use of experiments that make use of functioning prototypes of systems and involve the final users of the application. Experiments can be divided into *quantitative studies* and *qualitative studies* [56], based on the type of data collected. The technique used to collect quantitative data is the controlled experiment, while, for qualitative data, we have a wider range of options at our disposal, including interviews with users, direct observations, and focus groups.

8.3.2.1 Controlled Experiments

Examples of quantitative studies are the *controlled experiments* (also called *experimental studies*), defined in detail in some classic HCI texts such as [30]. These experiments aim to evaluate a certain system property by verifying a series of *hypotheses*, which can be confirmed (or infirmed) through a series of variables that can be measured quantitatively during the experiments performed by the users. The experiments have to be performed in a "controlled" environment, meaning that the person that coordinates the experiment has to systematically manipulate one or more conditions of the experiment (called *independent variables*), to study the effect of this change on other variables (*dependent variables*). The experiments should be conducted with a representative sample of users: the *test users*. During the experiment, the test users are asked to use the prototype to carry out a particular operation; at the same time, a series of "measurements" are carried out directly on the prototype or by observers (for example, notes are taken of the time required to complete a task, or the performance on accomplishing a specific task).

Controlled experiments can be useful for evaluating the functionality, effectiveness, and efficiency of a visual representation. Again, using the example that represents the messages exchanged between students of an online course (Fig. 2.6), to demonstrate that the visual representation is effective, the following hypothesis can be formulated:

> Lecturers of an online course that use the proposed graphical representations have a better knowledge of which students (1) are more active in posting messages on the forum, (2) read all the messages but don't actively participate in the discussions and (3) neither read nor write messages in the forum, compared to lecturers who use the traditional interfaces provided with the e-learning system without the support of visual representations.

To demonstrate this hypothesis, it is necessary to perform a series of experiments in which a number of dependent variables are measured. These variables have to be directly linked to the hypothesis that we wish to verify. We can define the following **dependent variables**:

1. knowledge of the students who are more active in initiating new *threads of discussion*;
2. knowledge of the students who have read the majority of the messages without consistently taking part in posting new messages;
3. knowledge of the students who have contributed to neither the reading nor the writing of messages in the forum.

To carry out a controlled experiment, the test users are split into two groups. One group uses the interfaces provided by the e-learning system, while the other uses the same interfaces but are aided by the visual representation that is being evaluated. Both groups of test users are requested to perform the same operations; the users' performance on the dependent variables is analyzed. The performance must be numerically measurable to be able to treat it with a statistical approach (calculating, for example, the average, variance, and standard deviation). Examples of performance can be the grade of accuracy with which each user responds to the questions or completes a particular operation (usually it is encoded with a real number between 0 and 1) or, in cases in which it is necessary to measure efficiency, the performance could be the time (in seconds) needed to answer a question or accomplish a specific task.

Another variant of controlled experiment involves two (or more) alternative solutions of graphical representations being compared empirically. This is useful when the project being worked on produces more than one solutions. In this case, the test users are divided into a number of groups, each group use a specific variant, and all groups carry out the same operations. The final analysis on the values measured in the empirical test indicate which proposal to choose.

8.3.2.2 Qualitative Methods

Qualitative evaluation methods are based on the collection of qualitative data from the test users, obtainable through questionnaires, interviews, and user monitoring. Qualitative methods differ from quantitative ones, described in the previous section, for the ability to analyze the phenomena from the user's point of view, rather than elaborating values measured in experiments. With qualitative methods, it is possible to evaluate the usefulness of a certain representation. Among these methods we can mention the *users' observation*, the *collection of the users' opinions*, and, finally, the *focus group*.

The users' observation consists of asking a certain number of test users to use the application's prototype and observe how users interact with it. Users can be asked to carry out some tasks, or to respond to a certain number of questions. In contrast to the controlled experiments, the aim of the observation consists of identifying possible problems that can rise when using the system; for example, a functionality that is not very clear or a certain visual mapping that could be interpreted incorrectly. This method involves a very expensive and engaging verification, particularly, when a large number of users is participating in the test.

Controlled experiments and the users' observations can be helpful when evaluating the functionality, efficiency, and effectiveness of the visual representations, but they are inappropriate for revealing problems that can manifest during the observations and for eliciting information on preference, impressions, and attitudes. The only way to understand if a certain visual representation can be useful for a certain type of user is to ask the user explicitly. A representation that provides a certain type of information very effectively and efficiently but that is of no use to users doesn't serve any purpose. For this reason, the **collection of the users' opinions** is a very important empirical technique, is relatively convenient, and can be carried out in various ways through interviews and questionnaires. Interviews are one of the most often used evaluation techniques in the social sciences, in market research, and also generally for other reasons in HCI. The key to the success of an evaluation based on interviews lies in the ability of interviewers to capture the most interesting comments from users. For example, to evaluate a certain visual representation, a number of users could be asked to use the prototype of the system, perhaps for a certain period of time, long enough to acquire a certain familiarity with the application. Successively, these users could be asked a certain number of predetermined questions, to obtain comments on general impression of the tool, their opinions on the facility of its use, its usefulness, etc.

A **focus group** is a technique that can help to investigate group attitudes, feelings, and beliefs of users on a proposed visual representation through group interviews [42, 46, 24, 25]. The interviews are carried out by bringing together a sample selection of test users and discussing as a group the functionalities offered by a visual representation. The conversation is led by a moderator, whose role is to facilitate the discussion, stimulate the interaction among participants, and keep the discussion focused on the aspects of the representation to be evaluated, besides collecting all participants' comments. The interesting aspect of this technique is that through the discussions and group interaction, in which each participant brings his or her own competence and personal experience, attention can be drawn to problems and situations that hadn't been foreseen during the system design. Prior to organizing a focus group, it is necessary to plan the meeting in detail: A demo has to be prepared in which the details of the system's functionalities are shown (unless these are already known); a video and audio recording system must be provided to be able to analyze the dialogues and interactions afterwards; the group of test users to involve and the number of focus group sessions to activate must be considered; finally, a series of questions must be prepared. The composition of the group of participants is a vital aspect, in terms of both the number and type of people. The ideal would be to have a group of potential users with a heterogeneous background, so as to cover every possible type of user. The number of participants is also a vital factor: Specialists in focus groups suggest groups of not less than 4 and not more than 12 participants per session. On the other hand, it is not easy to retrieve test users for this type of experiment, for which the composition of the group of participants is a compromise among the number of test users available, the competence and background of these users, and, finally, practical and logistic aspects. As to the questions to ask the group, it is necessary to prepare a number of questions that will elicit a series of critical comments on the representation.

8.4 Conclusion

We have dedicated this final chapter to an often neglected activity that should be part of every visual representation project: the empirical evaluation of the system conducted with potential users. A correct evaluation can reveal potential problems and indicate which actions have to be carried out to improve the quality of the visual representation. Empirical evaluations can be performed in the form of quantitative studies (such as controlled experiments) and qualitative studies (such as interviews), with the aim of providing some feedback on the functionality, effectiveness, efficiency, and usefulness of a visual representation.

References

1. Benjamin B. Bederson. Fisheye menus. In *Proceedings of ACM Conference on User Interface Software and Technology (UIST 2000)*, pages 217–225, 2000.
2. Benjamin B. Bederson, Jesse Grosjean, and Jon Meyer. Toolkit design for interactive structured graphics. *IEEE Transactions on Software Engineering*, 30(8):535–546, 2004.
3. Benjamin B. Bederson, Jon Meyer, and Lance Good. Jazz: An extensible zoomable user interface graphics toolkit in java. In *UIST '00: Proceedings of the 13th Annual ACM Symposium on User Interface Software and Technology*, pages 171–180. ACM, New York, 2000.
4. Benjamin B. Bederson, B. Shneiderman, and M. Wattenberg. Ordered and quantum treemaps: Making effective use of 2D space to display hierarchies. *ACM Transactions on Graphics*, 21(4):833–854, October 2002.
5. Jacques Bertin. *Graphics and Graphic Information Processing*. Walter de Gruyter, Berlin, 1981.
6. Mark Bruls, Kees Huizing, and Jarke J. van Wijk. Squarified treemaps. In *Proceedings of Joint Eurographics and IEEE TCVG Symposium on Visualization (TCVG 2000)*, pages 33–42. IEEE Press, 2000.
7. Tony Buzan and Barry Buzan. *The Mind Map Book*. BBC Active, 2006.
8. K. Stuart Card, Jock D. Mackinlay, and Ben Shneiderman. *Readings in Information Visualization: Using Vision to Think*. Morgan Kaufmann, San Francisco, 1999.
9. Chaomei Chen. Top 10 unsolved information visualization problems. *IEEE Computer Graphics and Applications*, 25(4):12–16, July-Aug. 2005.
10. Herman Chernoff. Using faces to represent points in k-dimensional space graphically. *Journal of the American Statistical Association*, 68(342):361–368, 1973.
11. W. S. Cleveland and R. McGill. Graphical perception: Theory, experimentation, and application to the development of graphical methods. *Journal of the American Statistical Association*, 79(387):531–554, 1984.
12. Donna Cox and Robert Patterson. Visualization study of the nsfnet. National Center for Supercomputing Applications (NCSA), 1994.
13. K. Cox, S. Eick, and T. He. 3D geographic network displays. *ACM SIGMOD Record*, 25(4):50–54, 1996.
14. Kenneth C. Cox, Stephen G. Eick, Graham J. Wills, and Ronald J. Brachman. Visual data mining: Recognizing telephone calling fraud. *Journal of Data Mining and Knowledge Discovery*, 1(2):225–231, 1997.
15. Kenneth Craik. *The Nature of Explanation*. Cambridge University Press, 1943.
16. A. Dix, J. Finlay, G. Abowd, and R. Beale. *Human–Computer Interaction*. Pearson Education, Prentice Hall, Harlow, 2nd edition, 1998.
17. P. Eades. A heuristic for graph drawing. *Congressus Numerantium*, 42:149–160, 1984.

18. K. M. Fairchild, S. E. Poltrock, and G. W. Furnas. Semnet: Three-dimensional graphic representation of large knowledge bases. In *Cognitive Science and its Application for Human-Computer Interface*. Raymonde Guindon (editor). Lawrence Erlbaum Associates, Hillsdale, NJ, 1988.

19. Stephen Few. *Show Me the Numbers. Designing Tables and Graphs to Enlighten*. Analytics Press, Oakland, CA, 2004.

20. Stephen Few. *Information Dashboard Design: The Effective Visual Communication of Data*. O'Reilly Media, Sebastopol, CA, 2006.

21. Ken Fishkin and Maureen C. Stone. Enhanced dynamic queries via movable filters. In *Proceedings of the SIGCHI Conference on Human Factors in Computing Systems*, pages 415–420, 1995.

22. T. Fruchterman and E. Reingold. Graph drawing by force-directed placement. *Software–Practice and Experience*, 21:1129–1164, 1991.

23. G. W. Furnas. Generalized fisheye views. In *Proceedings of the SIGCHI Conference on Human Factors in Computing Systems*, pages 18–23, 1986.

24. Anit Gibbs. Focus groups. *Social Research Update, University of Surrey, UK*, 1997. Num. 19. http://www.soc.surrey.ac.uk/sru/SRU19.html.

25. Thomas L. Greenbaum. *The Handbook for Focus Group Research*. Sage Publications, Thousand Oaks, CA, 1998.

26. J. Grosjean, C. Plaisant, and B. Bederson. Spacetree: supporting exploration in large node link tree, design evolution and empirical evaluation. In *Procedings of 2002 IEEE Symposium on Information Visualization*, pages 57–64, 2002.

27. Charles Hansen and Chris Johnson, editors. *Visualization Handbook*. Elsevier, Burlington, MA, 2004.

28. A Inselberg. *N*-dimensional graphics part I: Lines & hyperplanes. Technical report, IBM Scientific Center, Los Angeles, CA., 1981.

29. Robert Jacobson, editor. *Information Design*. MIT Press, Cambridge, MA, 1999.

30. Peter Johnson. *Human–Computer Interaction: Psycology, Task Analysis and Software Engineering*. McGraw-Hill, London, 1992.

31. Daniel Keim. Designing pixel-oriented visualization techniques: Theory and applications. *IEEE Transactions of Visualization and Computer Graphics*, 6(1), 2000.

32. Rob Kitchin and Martin Dodge. *Atlas of Cyberspace*. Pearson Education, Harlow, 2002.

33. Ernst Kleiberg, Huub van de Wetering, and J. J. van Wijk. Botanical visualization of huge hierarchies. In *Proceedings IEEE Symposium on Information Visualization (InfoVis'2001)*, pages 87–94, 2001.

34. Kurt Koffka. *Principles of Gestalt Psychology*. Harcourt, New York, 1935.

35. Wolfgang Köhler. *Gestalt Psychology*. Liveright, New York, 1929.

36. Robert Kosara, Fabian Bendix, and Helwig Hauser. Parallel sets: Interactive exploration and visual analysis of categorical data. *Parallel Sets: Interactive Exploration and Visual Analysis of Categorical Data*, 4(12), 2006.

37. John Lamping and Ramana Rao. The hyperbolic browser: A focus + context technique for visualizing large hierarchies. *Journal of Visual Languages and Computing*, 7(1):33–55, 1996.

38. J. H. Larkin and H. A. Simon. Why a diagram is (sometimes) worth ten thousand words. In J. Glasgow, H. Narayahan, and B. Chandrasekaram, editors, *Diagrammatic Reasoning–Cognitive and Computational Perspectives*, pages 69–109. AAAI Press, MIT Press, Cambridge, CA., 1995. Reprinted from Cognitive Science, 11:65–100, 1987.

39. J. D. Mackinlay. Automating the design of graphical presentations of relational information. *ACM Transactions on Graphics*, 5(2):110–141, 1986.

40. J. D. Mackinlay, G. G. Robertson, and S. K. Card. The perspective wall: Detail and context smoothly integrated. In *ACM Conference on Human Factors in Computing Systems (CHI '91)*, pages 173–179, 1991.

41. Riccardo Mazza. A graphical tool for monitoring the usage of modules in course management systems. In Pierre P. Levy, Benedicte Le Grand, Francois Poulet, Michel Soto, Laszlo Darago, Laurent Toubiana, and Jean-Francois Vibert, editors, *Pixelization Paradigm. Proceedings of VIEW2006*, LNCS, 4370, pages 164–172. Springer-Verlag, Berlin, 2007.

42. Riccardo Mazza and Alessandra Berre. Focus group methodology for evaluating information visualization techniques and tools. In *Proceedings of the 11th IEEE International Conference on Information Visualisation*, pages 74–80. IEEE Computer Society, 2007. http://doi.ieeecomputersociety.org/10.1109/IV.2007.51.

43. Riccardo Mazza and Vania Dimitrova. Coursevis: A graphical student monitoring tool for facilitating instructors in web-based distance courses. *International Journal in Human-Computer Studies (IJHCS)*, 65(2):125–139, February 2007. http://dx.doi.org/10.1016/j.ijhcs.2006.08.008.

44. George A. Miller. The magical number seven, plus or minus two. *The Psychological Review*, 63(2):81–97, 1956.

45. Tamara Munzner, Eric Hoffman, K. Claffy, and Bill Fenner. Visualizing the global topology of the mbone. In *Proceedings of the 1996 IEEE Symposium on Information Visualization*, pages 85–92, 1996.

46. J. Nielsen. The use and misuse of focus groups. *IEEE Software*, 14(1):94–95, January 1997.

47. Paul Potter. Ancient texts and the historian. *Journal of the CSHM/SCHM*, 7:169–176, 1990.

48. R. Rao and S. Card. The table lens: Merging graphical and symbolic representations in an interactive focus + context visualization for tabular information. In *ACM Conference on Human Factors in Software (CHI '94)*, 1994.

49. Harald Reiterer, Gabriela Tullius, and Thomas M. Mann. Insyder: A content-based visual-information-seeking system for the Web. *International Journal on Digital Libraries*, 5(1):25–41, 2005.

50. G. Robertson, J. Mackinlay, and S. Card. Cone trees: Animated 3D visualizations of hierarchical information. In *Proceedings of the SIGCHI Conference on Human Factors in Computing Systems: Reaching Through Technology*, pages 189–194, 1991.

51. B. Shneiderman. Tree visualization with treemaps: a 2D space-filling approach. *ACM Transactions on Graphics*, pages 92–99, 1991.

52. Ben Shneiderman. The eyes have it: A task by data type taxonomy for information visualizations. In *Proceedings of the 1996 IEEE Symposium on Visual Languages*, 1996.

53. R. Spence and M. D. Apperley. Data base navigation: An office environment for the professional. *Behaviour and Information Technology*, 1(1):43–54, 1982.

54. Robert Spence. *Information Visualisation*. Addison-Wesley, Reading, MA, 2001.

55. Robert Spence. *Information Visualisation, Design for Interaction*. Pearson Education, Harlow, 2nd edition, 2007.

56. M. Tory and T. Müller. Human factors in visualization research. *IEEE Transactions on Visualization and Computer Graphics*, 10(1), 2004.

57. Anne Treisman. Preattentive processing in vision. *Computer Vision, Graphics, and Image Processing*, 31(2):156–177, August 1985.

58. Edward R. Tufte. *The Visual Display of Quantitative Information*. Graphics Press, Cheshire, CT, 1983.

59. Edward R. Tufte. *Envisioning Information*. Graphics Press, Cheshire, CT, 1990.

60. Edward R. Tufte. *Visual Explanations*. Graphics Press, Cheshire, CT, 1997.

61. Edward R. Tufte. *Beautiful Evidence*. Graphics Press, Cheshire, CT, 2006.

62. L. Tweedie, B. Spence, D. Williams, and R. Bhogal. The attribute explorer. In *Conference on Human Factors in Computing Systems*, pages 435–436, 1994.

63. Jarke J. van Wijk and Huub van de Wetering. Cushion treemaps: Visualization of hierarchical information. In *IEEE Symposium on Information Visualization (INFOVIS'99)*, 1999.

64. M. O. Ward. Xmdvtool: Integrating multiple methods for visualizing multivariate data. In *Proceedings of IEEE Conference on Visualization*, 1994.

65. Colin Ware. *Information Visualization: Perception for Design*. Morgan Kaufmann, San Francisco, CA, 2nd edition, 2004.

66. Max Wertheimer. Untersuchungen zur lehre von der gestalt ii. *Psychologische Forschung*, 1923.

67. Graham J. Wills. Nicheworks–interactive visualization of very large graphs. *Journal of Computational and Graphical Statistics*, 8(2):190–212, 1999.

68. Jeremy M. Wolfe, Nicole Klempen, and Kari Dahlen. Postattentive vision. *Journal of Experimental Psychology: Human Perception and Performance*, 26(2):693–716, 2000.

Index

Printed in the United States of America